MY DETACHMENT

MY
DETACHMENT

—||—

A MEMOIR

TRACY KIDDER

RANDOM HOUSE
LARGE PRINT

For Judith Fuller, David Riggs,
and Sam Toperoff

Contents

AUTHOR'S NOTE

My Detachment is a personal history. I have thought it appropriate to change many of the names of people in this book. In some cases I have changed other identifying characteristics.

The following names are pseudonyms: Colonel Chamberlain, Major Great, First Sergeant Harb, Melvin Harris, Mr. Hatfield, Higgins, Joanie, Lieutenant Johnson, Colonel Robert Mahoney, Mary Anne, Nat, Lieutenant Stan Pease, Lieutenant Colonel Dean Riddle, Rose, Mike Rosenthal, Schulzie, Sergeant Stoney Spikes, and Tex.

SUNDAE and SORTIE are invented code-words, replacing the actual ones.

Special thanks to Stuart Dybek, Kate Medina, and Richard Todd.

Thanks also to the Rockefeller Foundation for a residency at the Bellagio Study and Conference Center, where a draft of this book was completed.

MY DETACHMENT

WAR STORIES

I AM THE AUTHOR OF **IVORY FIELDS**, A NOVEL. I wrote it soon after I came home from Vietnam. Not many have read the book. After thirty-three publishers turned it down, I lit a fire in a trash barrel behind a rented house in Iowa and burned up all my copies of the manuscript. Years and years went by, and the book became a part of my distant memories of being a soldier, memories that would creep up on me when I was washing dishes or turning a key in a lock, memories that I wished away. Then one morning another copy of the novel arrived in the mail, from an old friend who was cleaning out his files, and I realized I was glad to have it back. From time to time I look at it, and I think.

The protagonist of **Ivory Fields** is a strange, doomed young Army officer named Larry Dempsey. He's a second lieutenant, just as I was when I arrived in Vietnam in June 1968. But Lieutenant Dempsey is sent to Vietnam to lead an infantry platoon in combat. Whereas I commanded, in a manner of speaking, a detachment of eight enlisted men who performed an indoor sort of job, a classified mission called communications intelligence, in support of the 198th Light Infantry Brigade of the Americal Division. We belonged to the Army Security Agency, but in Vietnam we worked under the false though actually more descriptive name Radio Research.

I imagine this disguise was meant to confuse not only our enemies but also our friends who didn't have proper security clearances, but I don't know what difference it made. Our compounds were off limits to most American soldiers, and we never saw the Vietcong or North Vietnamese. At higher headquarters in Chu Lai and in small airplanes, other radio research soldiers listened in on the enemy's encrypted Morse code communications, and what they learned—mainly locations— was passed to my detachment, and passed on by me to the brigade commander. I remember an article in an overseas edition of **Time** that accurately described what units like ours were doing. I read the article in my hootch, in my detachment's compound, which was tucked inside the brigade's fortified base camp, Landing Zone Bayonet. The camp was situated at the edge of the coastal plain, at the base of the foothills of the central highlands, in the part of South Vietnam that the American authorities had labeled I Corps. I spent most of my year at LZ Bayonet, inside the perimeter.

I remember watching a small group of American soldiers head out one evening. The selections that memory makes often puzzle me, but I probably remember seeing the patrol because it was the closest I ever got to the infantry in Vietnam. I was standing on the hill near my detachment's antennas. I could see most of the base camp and to the west, out beyond the bunkers and barbed wire, green hills with taller hills like a wall behind them, and on a rock face in white paint, ALPHA $\frac{1}{46}$ THE GUNFIGHTERS, the name of an infantry company that must have passed through in the course of the war and left that memento behind. The sun was setting on the hilltops, below great-chested clouds, and I was gazing out that way, glad to be apart from my men for a while, when I caught sight of the infantry patrol on one of the intervening hills, a group of olive-drab figures in procession, tiny at that distance, humpbacked beneath rucksacks. It would be dark soon. They were trudging away from the camp at an hour when I would have wanted to be heading in the opposite direction, toward hootches and beer and cots and mosquito nets and generators.

I had decided that this war was wrong. Not because of anything I had read recently or because of what I had seen so far. I opposed the war mainly because a lot of my friends were protesting against it back home. I watched the patrol with morbid fascination, with something like the feeling I used to get as a boy when I'd inch toward the edge of the roof of my grandmother's apartment building in New York, until the soldiers went over the hill in single file and disappeared.

I was glad I wasn't going with them. But what if I had to? What if I enraged some field grade officer and for punishment got reassigned to the infantry? A fluttery sensation passed through my chest, and for a moment my hands felt weak. I imagined my civilian friends watching me. I imagined my girl-friend, Mary Anne. She might approve of my being less than gung ho, but not homesick and frightened. I had let some of those feelings slip into a few letters, and she had written me a sweet but keep-your-chin-up letter in which she'd said, "Don't be so paranoid." I'd be more careful from now on. Soon my letters would suggest a stoical, even at times heroic young fellow. And after all, here I was, standing on the edge of the dangerous highlands under an operatic Asian sky, in a situation she ought to find poignant, a reluctant commander drawing hazardous duty pay.

I wandered down the hill, past our latrine, toward the enlisted men's hootches, and turned in at the one we had made into our lounge. Outside the screen door, I heard beer cans hissing open. I went inside as usual. Five or six of my men were sitting around the TV set, awaiting that evening's episode of **Combat!** The title filled the screen: "What Are the Bugles Blowin' For?" Sergeant Saunders's platoon has volunteered for a dangerous mission, which takes them, through the pouring rain, into a bombed-out village in France. The one kid left in the village joins up with them. He wants to fight the Krauts, too, because they killed his sister. He wants to get the man who did it, so he keeps checking the faces of the Krauts that Sergeant Saunders's squad guns down. Sergeant Saunders is brave and wise, and kind to children and women, especially nuns.

I had a good sergeant, a buck sergeant in his early twenties, three stripes on the sleeves. His name was Stoney Spikes, and he came from Alabama. He had a strong face, with a big square chin, and the other men obeyed him. He kept one of his two pairs of jungle boots polished, more or less, for the inspections we occasionally endured, which were for me almost a form of combat. The other pair he left unshined, at first perhaps because he saw no sense in shining them and later on, I think, because they made him feel more like the soldier he wished he was—because a real soldier, an infantryman, a grunt, would never wear shiny boots in the bush. Spikes had gone away on leave and had run into some buck sergeants his age who had Combat Infantryman's Badges. "They got a name for people like us, Lieutenant," he told me when he came back. His jaw hardened. The term was REMF. It stood for "Rear Echelon Mother Fucker." Spikes never seemed quite the same after he found out what real soldiers thought of soldiers like us. In my memory, he sits forever in the lounge, at the end of another hot and dusty day. He opens a beer and tells the other men to hush as **Combat!** fills the TV screen, and he is dressed for the show in those sad, scuffed jungle boots.

IN A SENSE, I PUT ON SCUFFED BOOTS TOO, WHEN I came home and began to write my novel about an infantry platoon and its lieutenant. Writing about experiences that I didn't have in Vietnam quieted real memories. A decade later, I had become a magazine writer. In 1978, still curious about those experiences that I had merely imagined, I traveled around the country, interviewing

Vietnam combat veterans, to gather material for an article. And what a lot of strange and violent experience had been transported back into the United States, into jails and treatment centers and much more often into houses on quiet, tree-lined streets. I met a former infantryman who remembered getting a black eye when a piece of his best friend's skull hit him in the face, a former combat medic who had finally weaned himself from morphine but still had lurid dreams about the men whose lives he hadn't saved, a government official who had lost an arm and both legs to a hand grenade, and dozens of others with terrible stories, all certifiable.

Also, in Louisville, Kentucky, I met a man whom I'll call Bill, who told me a different kind of story, a tale about a tale.

In a bar one night, after listening to a bunch of other Vietnam veterans tell war stories, Bill had said, "We were ridin' on an APC outside Pleiku, when we got hit." Bill had told the barroom that he could still see those tracer rounds, like little red-tailed comets coming at them from the tree line, and the way his buddy who was sitting beside him on the armored personnel carrier slumped over and, as if in slow motion, fell by the side of the trail. Bill was scared, he told the bar. Fuckin' A, who wouldn't be? But that was his buddy, that was a GI lying wounded and dying back there on the trail. The captain, though, was yelling at the driver to **di di mao.** And Bill was yelling at the captain that they had to go back, and the coward told him to shut up and shouted at the driver again to **move out.** So afterward, back in base camp, the captain, to cover his ass, busted Bill to spec. 4, and Bill brooded and brooded and finally made up his mind to get payback. He had to kill the officer. He had to frag the lifer.

Bill was sitting on a sofa in his parents' living room when he described himself telling that story. He said that he really did experience some moments of near combat in Vietnam, and that there really was a captain he wanted to kill, who busted him in rank. And in fact, Bill came home wounded. But his actual offense was repeated drunkenness, and he got his wound when he fell in a hole in a base camp and a friend, also stumbling drunk, fell in on top of him and broke his jaw. Bill had come home feeling miserable and had moved between the city's drunk tank and its barrooms, where he told his story again and again. "It just came out one time, and it felt really good. Then each time I'd say it, I'd make it a little more glorified," Bill told me. "When I came home, the other veterans always had big wild stories, and I didn't have anything like theirs to tell. And theirs was probably as fictitious as mine." He looked down at his hands and seemed to smile at them.

"It takes the place of things you didn't do. After a while, if you tell 'em enough, the ones people like to hear, you almost start to believe them."

When one considers the suffering of actual combatants and the much more numerous sufferings of Vietnamese civilians, it seems like sheer perversity for a rear-echelon soldier to come home wishing his experiences more dreadful than they were. But Bill was not alone. Most of the American soldiers who went to Vietnam were boys, whether they were twenty-two or just eighteen. They had watched a lot of movies and TV. I'm sure that many set out for Vietnam feeling confused or unhappy, as adolescents tend to do, and deep down many probably thought they would return with improved reasons for feeling that way. But of the roughly three million Americans who went to the war dressed as soldiers, only a small minority returned with Combat Infantryman's Badges, certain proof of a terrible experience. Imagine all the bullshit stories Vietnam inspired.

My own wasn't exactly a story, just a freighted suggestion. I made it twice, the last time on a night in the mid-1970s. I got drunk at a Christmas party. Afterward, imagining that I'd been insulted by the various people I'd insulted there, I started crying angrily in the backseat of my car. A friend was driving. He asked me what was wrong, and I felt the need for a better explanation than the real one, whatever the real one was. My friend knew I'd been in Vietnam. "Did you ever kill anyone, buddy?" I said.

"No," he said. "Did you?"

"I don't want to talk about it."

Ivory Fields was a more elaborate war story. In late 1968, just back from Vietnam, I sat down at a table in my parents' house, and I began:

> When we were there things were on the increase, not the wane. The coonskin cap was still nailed on the walls of Cam Ranh Bay, so to speak.
>
> About this time is when the sad story begins. It is the saddest story you ever hope to hear.

THE TABOR'S SOUND

I THINK I EXPECTED READERS TO VIEW MY NOVEL as autobiographical, and I was also beginning to sculpt my memories, looking for configurations that would make me more comfortable with them. I gave the lieutenant in **Ivory Fields** a "pained and hawklike face" and a sketchy past. His father isn't mentioned. His mother appears only briefly and is described as "once birdlike, but rounder poultry these days." No one who knew me could have imagined I meant to depict my own thin, beautiful, high-strung mother. Lieutenant Dempsey's experiences in the war are also very different, of course—analogous to mine perhaps, but much more dramatic, the big shadows on the wall looming over me. For one thing, he gets shot to death. (He is done in by a conniving sergeant and a giant black soldier named Ivory Fields; he dies while trying to protect, in his bumbling way, a Vietnamese girl whom his men have raped.)

A reader might well think that the traits Dempsey and I had in common were fiction and at the same time imagine that some of Dempsey's fictional experiences resembled mine. Imagining the book's reception, I could see myself denying that I had suffered as he does. The more I demurred, the more the reader would think of me, He must have seen **some stuff** over there.

When my novel begins, Dempsey is already an infantry lieutenant on his way to Vietnam. He goes for patriotic reasons. He assumes the war is just. My case was more mystifying, at least to me.

I grew up in the town of Oyster Bay, on the north shore of Long Island, at a time when the great suburban expansion had only just begun. Our house had been the gardener's cottage of a huge estate. It sat on several green acres, beside one of the island's last big hardwood forests. I spent what seems to me a very pleasant childhood playing with my two brothers and our friends at the foot of huge oaks and among pear trees and flowering dogwoods and on the waters of Long

Island Sound. We carved our initials and later our first girlfriends' initials as well into the elephant-like skin of beech trees. I had a fierce temper as a child. Its eruptions sometimes made me climb into bed with my shoes on at midday. I had an equally fierce fear of the dark, which made real bedtimes dreadful, until I was ten or eleven and imaginary snakes stopped crawling up the gray stucco walls and through the window that looked out over the field in front of the house.

My mother was a locally famous high school English teacher. My father was a New York City lawyer. I never sensed while growing up that his career was a disappointment to him, but I knew that he had relished his years in the Pacific in World War II. He had a collection of stories, which he loved to tell and which, as the years went on, I liked more and more to hear. The stories about his chief petty officer, who was wonderfully competent at sea and always got so drunk ashore he'd have to be carted back to the ship in a wheel-barrow. The story about the time my father talked his hulking mess attendant into dropping the carving knife with which he'd been chasing the cook around the galley. And the story about a Christmas Eve when the ship he commanded was patrolling the American side of the Strait of Juan de Fuca, and the commander of the Canadian corvette patrolling the other side suggested that they raft the vessels together and have a Christmas party. My father, though fearing court-martial, agreed. (Drinking was allowed on the Canadian ship, not on my father's American one, so there was a lot of traffic back and forth during the party, and all of Christmas after the ships parted ways, they exchanged semaphore signals: Did the Yanks know the whereabouts of a certain Canadian chief boatswain's mate? Had the Canadians come across an American chief petty officer, perhaps sleeping it off in one of their lifeboats?)

Earlier in the war, my father served as executive officer on a minesweeper. The ship was headed for the battle of Tarawa, but at the last moment they were sent elsewhere. "It was kind of a gyp," my father would say. When I was a child and heard him tell this story, I'd imagine him standing on the bridge, watching the lucky battle fleet recede as his own ship sailed away from action. I shared his disappointment for years, even as a teenager, although by then I'd also think, What if he'd gone to Tarawa? Would I still exist?

He was shy around my brothers and me but didn't seem to care if we saw him kiss my mother or heard him call her "sweetheart." Walking to school alone one day, I realized I must have been adopted. I didn't look like him. I had brown hair, not black. I was already taller. And he rarely lost his temper. I resembled pictures of my mother's father, though—the long French nose, the high forehead, the myopic eyes. I went off alone into the woods to have my secret fantasies about who my father really was. My own was both too ordinary and too odd.

My mother told us we were "middle class," a claim most of that post–World War II generation of Americans, especially those on either end of the middle, seemed afraid **not** to make. Her own family had been well-to-do, and then, when she was still a girl, her father's business failed. A year or two later he died, and they lived on the charity of relatives and the wages of my mother's oldest brother.

As for my father, he wasn't rich compared to most of his friends, but the place where he saw wealthier people was the yacht club. Naturally, my mother liked to spend money, and just as predictably, my father hated parting with it. Every week she put a little something from the grocery money into the Christmas Club at the A & P. This was fortunate. My father one Christmas morning presented to my older brother and me a bunch of underwear he had bought at one of his favorite Manhattan stores. We opened the packages and found T-shirts with one sleeve missing and with outlandishly long waists, long as dresses, all with "Factory Reject" stamped on them. My brother and I looked at each other but didn't protest until he was out of earshot. We knew he meant the gifts sincerely. He bought his suits at discount stores—two pairs of pants for the price of one. He once gave a New York City cabdriver a ten-cent tip and the man threw it back at him, and when I asked him how that made him feel, my father said, "Well, I was glad to have my dime back." He didn't want my mother to have her own bank account. As a rule, he was grumpy only once a month, when paying the household bills himself. "Do you know your mother hides them from me?" he asked me one time, with puzzled consternation. But we never wanted for anything essential, and he spent freely on our educations. I went to public school through eighth grade, then to boarding school, Andover, and then, like my father, to Harvard, where he sent me a handsome allowance, which I sometimes squandered on backgammon losses and once on a handmade suit.

WHEN I WAS A BOY, MY FATHER BOUGHT A CAT-boat, thirty feet long and fifty years old, named the **Mayflower**. A tub, my brothers and I called it. If the original **Mayflower** had sailed as slowly, I thought, the English would never have made it to Plymouth. Every summer when his vacation began, he and my mother and brothers and I would climb aboard and head down Long Island Sound for Woods Hole in Cape Cod, my father shedding his business suit, getting down to his underwear by the time the sail was hoisted. He had equipped the boat with an Army surplus ice chest that had been used to store plasma. HUMAN BLOOD, it read on the side. The boat's foghorn had been a birthday present to my mother, who forgave him but never forgot. I remember sitting in the cockpit under a leaky awning, at anchor in a muddy little harbor, the rain beating down. I was slapping mosquitoes and grumbling when my father reached over and tapped me gently on the knee and said, without irony, "What could be nicer!"

He had spent his summers in Woods Hole as a boy, and his tiny, eccentric mother still kept a large, chaotic house there. One night, when most of her twenty-six grandchildren and their parents sat down to dinner, my younger cousins all yelling and running around the table, poking the adults' butts with forks, the little old lady at the head of the table bowed her head and softly intoned, "Lord, please help us safely through this meal." I felt more embarrassed than amused, as if the girl I dreamed about were watching from the doorway.

On a summer day in Woods Hole when I was thirteen, my parents had brought some friends along for a picnic on the **Mayflower.** These friends had a summer place in the town and several daughters, one about my age, Mary Anne. I studied her in glances. She had curly hair braided in pigtails and was laughing. As soon as she and her family came aboard, I started acting every bit the mariner, raising the sail, trimming the sheet. Soon we were lumbering slowly up Vineyard Sound. Continuing my exertions, I cut my elbow. I went down to the cabin, where Mary Anne had also gone to have a look around. We were alone. I found the Band-Aids and asked her to put one on my cut. She did. "Could you put another on?" I asked.

How my spirits would lift all the rest of the years of my adolescence on the last leg of my family's voyages, coming down Vineyard Sound before a following wind, the **Mayflower**'s mast and boom, thick as a pair of old telephone poles, creaking under full sail, and soon Woods Hole and Mary Anne's house heaving into view. I saw her in the summers. Sometimes we wrote to each other in the off-seasons. Her interest in me ebbed and flowed, and mine in her, but mine never fell as far as hers. The craving for distinction that I began to feel was always there underneath the hope of making her admire me, and after disappointments I'd feel as if I still had her to hope for, or at least a letter in my box in the mailroom at Andover, a letter in a blue envelope, which I'd study in my room, searching until I thought I'd found, in the news about her, news about her affection for me.

My parents had always called me by my middle name, which was my mother's maiden name—Tracy. It was an unusual given name in those days, and my first year at Andover, wanting to be different from the boy I used to be, I decided to switch to my first name, John. When I came home that summer, a report card with D's in math and science and this note from my housemaster followed:

> Where John's natural aptitude will serve, he can polish off assignments, but when real difficulty is faced, he is likely to shirk. . . . The Junior Physical Education program report substantiates our own observations. They credit him with working very hard—usually; he did well in gymnastics and in track, where he has definite aptitudes. They note, "Whenever the going got real tough and it involved real courage, he would not proceed with any test."

I reverted to my middle name the following year, and I didn't get another bad report card until basic training, when the officer in charge of the platoon, another sort of housemaster, gave me, on the standard form, a mediocre grade in "Moral Courage." I went to him and said, "I resent this, sir." He told me that he didn't mean to impugn my morals or my courage. He gave me the grade because I'd gotten flustered when leading the platoon in close-order drill and had sent them marching in two different directions.

I remember standing, at thirteen, in the study of my Andover housemaster, asking for help with algebra and then becoming so afraid that the severe look on his face would turn into something worse that I lost track of everything he said until he started yelling that I wasn't paying attention. I remember this with a vividness that surprises me, a measure of how infrequently I was mistreated as a boy. The masters liked to say that at Andover students enjoyed "complete freedom tempered by expulsion." But I remember assigned seats at daily chapel and a master in the balcony recording the names of absentees, and punishments for missing chapel or church on Sundays or for getting a few bad grades.

What the masters actually granted us students, maybe out of laziness or maybe by design, was license with one another. Out of four years of daily sermons, I don't remember one, or any other adult intervention, that addressed the cruelty within the student body. There were only two

Asians in my class. One was a small, lonely Chinese boy. Passing him, some of my classmates would pull their eyelids outward with their fingers and say, "My name Charlie Chan." After a few months at Andover, he disappeared and was found three days later hiding in the rafters of the music building.

There were other victims. I joined in the hazing of several. Of course I was afraid of being ostracized myself, but I was over six feet tall and a good athlete, in spite of nearsightedness. During one baseball game freshman year, a fly ball hit me on the head, but I was teased about it for only a day or two because earlier that game I'd hit two home runs. Besides, I was good at football, the ultimate immunity. I felt as though I lived for the local prestige of playing football and for its licensed violence, but my chief ambition those four years was getting through that school.

I got good grades in history and Spanish, and the summer after graduation I saw Marlon Brando in **The Ugly American**. It made a strong impression. America, I realized, was in the midst of a great struggle with the Soviet Union, a struggle between democracy and tyranny, which we Americans would lose unless we learned to present our case properly to the lesser nations. So I would become a diplomat. Harvard was a good place to start. At Harvard, the major in political science was called "Government," and Harvard had produced a lot of those who did govern us, including President Kennedy, of course. I had been in Cambridge only a few months when he was assassinated. All over Harvard Yard, students streamed from the doorways of the freshman dorms. I stood among a group outside Wigglesworth Hall. Someone had a portable radio. President Johnson had just been sworn in, and we listened as he declared that America would honor her commitments from somewhere or other all the way to "Vietnam"—the last syllable rhyming with **ma'am.** Someone in that crowd of freshmen said it was a great relief to hear this, and looking back, I see faces nodding in agreement—as I was—faces that, three and four years later, were chanting, "Hell no, we won't go!"

I had spent my four years at Andover without much access to girls or alcohol. In Cambridge, I had no problem getting alcohol, at the Varsity Liquor Store in Harvard Square, with my fake Montana driver's license. Girls were harder to come by. I drank a lot, and I read Marx and Engels, Locke and Rousseau, Hobbes and Kant. I studied introductory economics and American pressure-group politics. I wrote a hopelessly muddled paper about agriculture in Argentina. And just for fun, I took a creative writing course. The first stories I wrote—there was one about a girl who looked like a duck, but a good-looking duck—contained some plausible dialogue, and the instructor liked them. More important, so did some of the young women in the class. Here, it seemed, was a way to meet and impress girls.

Sophomore year, on the strength of those first short stories, I got into a writing seminar taught by Robert Fitzgerald, the poet and translator of Homer. The class convened in a long, narrow room in the ancient Sever Hall, no doubt renovated many times, and unadorned. A window looked out on Harvard Yard, the snow and leafless trees against dark brick and stone. The messages in architecture were mostly hidden from me but not unfelt. I loved the plainness of that room long before I realized that I did. But I felt that I was being inducted into something old and important as soon as Mr. Fitzgerald entered the room.

He was a small man in his early sixties. He wore a beret and carried a green cloth book bag. He sat down at the head of the long seminar table and then eyed each of us. He had a pair of reading glasses, half-glasses. He lowered them and, looking at us over the rims, he said, "The only reason for writing is to produce something **classic**. And I expect that you will produce **classic** work during this term."

He let that sink in, then double-jabbed a finger at the wastebasket beside him. "The greatest repository I know of for writers. And I do hope that it will **precede** me."

During the first part of every class, he would talk about the craft of writing and read aloud to us, occasionally a student's poem or story, and more often works by famous writers he had known. He read us a story by his old friend Flannery O'Connor and said when he finished, "That story unwinds like a Rolex watch." In the second half of every class, he had us write. He warmed us up, then made us exercise, and somehow I could always write something in that room for him. In his presence, even poetry seemed possible. Mr. Fitzgerald insisted I try a poem now and then. I struggled and finally got one off that he seemed to like. It came back from him with this comment at the bottom: "This is very like a poem."

I wrote story after story, sometimes two a week. I set one at boarding school and depicted a pair of boys: a popular one who feels stirrings of compassion for another who is tormented by his classmates. It had a certain complexity; the tormented boy is truly obnoxious. I called it "The Tabor's Sound," after a line from Wordsworth. I stayed up two entire nights to write it, then showed it to a friend. He'd been to prep school, too, and was trying to write about the experience himself. "Your story stinks," he said. This was the first and at the time the only literary friend I'd acquired, and I thought him very wise and perspicacious, because once he had encouraged me. After he pointed out my story's flaws, I saw them clearly, too. But I decided to leave the thing in Mr. Fitzgerald's box, just so he'd know that I was working.

I was in my seat when he walked into class a few days later. I always arrived early. "It's not a fit day out for man nor beast," Mr. Fitzgerald said and stamped the snow off his galoshes. Then he greeted us as usual, first with a smile, and then with a sigh, as he heaved his green book bag onto the table. Mr. Fitzgerald's green bag contained our poems and stories, **my** story, with his comments written on them. I could not have been more interested in that book bag if Mr. Fitzgerald had been our guardian, returning with food he'd found out in the world. But the way he sighed as he heaved his sack onto the table insinuated that what lay inside wasn't as valuable as food. Certainly it looked like a heavy load for one professor to carry.

"I'm going to read a story by one of the writers in this class, a story I particularly liked," he said. "It's called 'The Tabor's Sound.' " He lowered his glasses and looked around the room. "I assume that all of you know where the phrase comes from." Suddenly the mellifluous voice that had read to us from the likes of James Agee and Wallace Stevens and Flannery O'Connor was reading my story. He'd made it through several sentences before I realized that my mouth was hanging open. I closed it fast. I hoped no girls had noticed. I wanted to ask Mr. Fitzgerald to stop. Then I wished he never would.

Mary Anne had come to Boston that year for college. We had gone on a couple of dates. On each I felt as if I were looking in a mirror, trying desperately to find the angle where my face would become handsome. These were the first times I had seen her away from Woods Hole, and I felt lost without the things we had in common, without the sea and sailboats. The pigtails had turned into a complicated bun, from which small curls escaped, like jewels on her neck. I wished I could touch them, tracing their spirals with a finger. She wore small pearl earrings. She was animated as always, but now her silly name for me—Tray-Tray—came out with an extra touch of irony. She laughed and then bent over and slapped herself on the thighs, just as I remembered her doing. She'd always made exaggerated movements, pantomiming mirth or horror or grave injury. When she made herself look awkward, it only reminded me of her gracefulness.

"So what have you been up to?" I asked.

"Oh, a bit of this, a bit of that," she said, with a closed-lipped smile and her eyebrows lifting.

Well, I could be mysterious, too. Maybe I'd

been up to dangerous, adult things myself. I made up a story about a girl, a casual liaison. She'd given me a venereal disease, I said, in a low voice, trying to imitate Mary Anne's smile.

She smiled back, but without her usual certainty.

I hadn't seen her much since then. But I called her often at the pay phone in her dorm, dialing again and again to get past the busy signal. Then I'd read my latest story. I had told her I was going to be a writer. I knew she approved. I didn't imagine her listening in a hot phone booth while other students banged on the door. That wouldn't have stopped me anyway. Occasionally I'd hear her yawn but would read on undeterred. I called her up that night after Fitzgerald's class and read her "The Tabor's Sound."

"Oh," she said about half an hour later. "I **like** that."

"Did you really like it?"

"Yes, of course. I did, I really did. Now I have to get some sleep."

A few days later, I quit studying government. My first writing teacher had told me that I shouldn't major in English, because if I wanted to be a writer I ought to learn about something besides literature so as to have something to write about. But I didn't believe that anymore. I didn't think a writer should be interested in politics. I certainly wasn't interested in the sort taught at Harvard. I was reading fiction, consuming it at a rate I've never equaled since: Dickens and George Eliot, Henry James and Emily Brontë, Faulkner and F. Scott Fitzgerald and Hemingway—all of Hemingway, who gave me the concept of the writer as himself a hero. Meanwhile, I'd acquired a sleep disorder and an assigned-reading disability. I couldn't read any book that was on an official reading list, and I stayed up all night writing stories for Mr. Fitzgerald and went to sleep around the time my classes in government began.

Henry Kissinger taught one of those, a course in the political history of World War II. He was just another professor, not famous yet. I had gone to only a few classes. "France was a de-**morel**-ized nation after World War I," he kept explaining. One day I straggled into the lecture hall and found that something else was going on, a debate of sorts, Kissinger at the podium, graduate students in the audience politely arguing with him. A student friend whispered to me that Kissinger had given over this lecture period to argue about the Vietnam War. "The conflict," it was called. The debate was very polite and academic, and puzzling to me. I listened for a while, then whispered to my friend, "I'm getting out of here. I'm going to go major in English." I picked up my books and slipped out of the room. I didn't stick around long enough to get the hang of either side of the argument. One should always stay at least that long.

ON A VISIT HOME, I STOPPED IN AT MR. BERNstein's store, where my mother had always bought my clothes. Mr. Bernstein had followed my life's progress with his measuring tape while cracking jokes. But when I came in that day, to present myself, a finished product now, this old friend of my youth was subdued. Leaning an elbow on a pile of chinos, he said that Oyster Bay had just lost its first boy in Vietnam. "He was a nice kid. A good-looking kid," he said, gazing out his store window. "A thirty-four waist, thirty-one leg." I thought I'd remember that line, for a story. I didn't hear much of anything about Vietnam for months after that.

In the fall of 1964, Cambridge was still more a town than a university's metropolis, and its present seemed firmly connected with its past. Many stores and restaurants around Harvard Square were pleasantly unkempt: the Hayes-Bickford and the grubby Waldorf cafeteria, where you could go for a snack late at night; Felix's newsstand, where you could get a shoeshine and in the back room buy a girlie magazine. At the Wursthaus, you could have a lunch of heavy breaded meat with your visiting father, as I did with mine and as he had done with his father twenty-five years before. The rules at Harvard hadn't changed much. A student could still be expelled, for instance, if he was caught with a girl in his room outside of what were called "parietal hours." In the spring of freshman year, I had wandered down to the banks of the Charles River to join a student protest. The upperclassmen had taken up this chant: "Two-four-six-eight, let the sycamores foliate." The city had planned to cut down some of the trees along the river. A dean arrived and told the crowd to break it up, and we obeyed.

The large antiwar protests hadn't begun, and not much accurate reporting was coming yet from Vietnam. To the students who cared about politics, what seemed to matter most just then was civil rights, and many leaders of that movement still kept a discreet silence on the war. Styles were changing, of course, but one still had to wear a jacket and tie to eat at one's house or social club. Girls wore stiff, nubbly, high-necked dresses to mixers. The Beatles had long hair, but long hair then merely impinged on the ears. I was very surprised when a student acquaintance of mine grew a beard. "Why would you want to have one of those things?" someone asked him at lunch.

He put up a spirited defense. "I think you have to be lacking basic curiosity not to wonder how you'd look in a beard," he said.

Most of my roommates were former prep school boys, and most of the other students I knew belonged to the A.D. Club, one of Harvard's social clubs. The A.D. was less prestigious than the Porcellian, Harvard's rough equivalent of Skull and Bones at Yale, but it was old and some of its student members were already millionaires. I was invited to join my sophomore year, probably by mistake. A few months later, one of the older undergraduate members had told me, "You're the wrong Kidder." That is, my family wasn't part of the Wall Street brokerage.

The exclusivity of clubs was denounced by some students and faculty, who were of course snobbish in their own ways—this was Harvard after all. One other club at least seemed to care about the criticism. They were about to admit a black member. "I think it's a good idea," an elderly classics professor, a graduate member of the A.D. Club, said one day at lunch. He smiled. "But I'm glad it's **they** who are doing it." He used to stop in regularly, especially during the "punching season" (the period when new members were considered), and he'd recommend certain students he'd been keeping an eye on, always former public school boys. He felt the club should always have a few of those.

I was pretty sure a writer shouldn't belong to an organization like the A.D. Usually I hesitated and looked around to see who might be watching before I turned my key in the door and passed from a narrow side street of Cambridge into the spacious clubhouse. It had a Picasso on one wall, and many wood-paneled, tall-ceilinged, leather-upholstered chambers, and a poolroom, where under the inscription HE WHO LOSETH HIS LIFE SHALL FIND IT hung old photographs of former clubmen in World War I uniforms. Opposition to the Vietnam War didn't run high there. I think most of us assumed that whatever the ruling class of America did was essentially correct, for the simple reason that we belonged to that class. I don't remember hearing any talk about deferments from the draft; all college students were still deferred.

Anyway, I was preoccupied. I kept expecting Mr. Fitzgerald to read a story of mine to the class again. I gave him one I knew he'd like. When I came into his office for a private conference, he was puffing on the stub of a cigarette. He'd put himself on short rations and was making each one last. He had a copy of the **Iliad** opened on his desk. Looking up from it, he said, "I should never have tried to do both the **Odyssey** and this. It's too much for an old man."

I thought, You aren't old! But I didn't dare to say so. Anyway, I wanted to hear about my story. I asked him, in a voice already exulting at his answer, "How did you like that story of mine, Mr. Fitzgerald?"

He performed his ritual of the reading glasses, pulling them an inch down his nose and looking at me over the the rims. "Not much," he said.

He was right. I wasn't performing well, though not for lack of trying or, God knows, desire. I had become self-conscious about writing. I started a novel. I wrote twenty pages or so, but the most interesting parts were the comments and little drawings I made in the margins, and created with greater care than anything in the actual text, imagining my biographer's delight in finding them. All of the stories I wrote in my room late at night, and the pastiches I wrote in class, came back with brief comments such as "Okay but no flash," in an elegantly penned script. Mr. Fitzgerald had talked to us about something he called "the luck of the conception." Now I knew what he meant. Several times that fall I had a dream in which I'd come upon the perfect story. The dream didn't contain the story itself, just the fact that I possessed it. It was a dream suffused with joy, and I awoke from it with the same kind of sorrow I felt when I thought of Mary Anne.

I dreamed about her, too. In one of those dreams, another Harvard guy came up to me and said, "Mary Anne? **Everyone** knows her." I woke up feeling that I'd been sent a message. She'd been too busy to go out with me. Back then people spoke of "playing the field." Mary Anne wouldn't have used that phrase, but it described what she was doing, I believed.

I often went to the A.D. Club to drink away my sorrows. One evening a couple of older members sat down with me. After several glasses of bourbon and water, I declared, "I'm the best goddamn writer at Harvard."

I remember scornful smiles. "Are you aware of the works of Voltaire?" one of them asked me. "And of a certain character named Candide?"

I hadn't read Voltaire, so I didn't get his reference. I claimed that I had read it. Then they quizzed me, and proved I hadn't. I punched one of them in the face. A brief scuffle followed. We knocked over the grandfather clock and broke a lot of glasses. In the aftermath, during the reconciliation, I explained to the other young man, the one I hadn't punched, that my girlfriend had dumped me. He said, of the undergraduate I'd just fought with, "Yes, well, his mother died two months ago." Then I felt chastened. His grief was probably just as keen as mine.

IN THE SUMMER OF 1965, BEFORE MY JUNIOR year, I'd driven to Mexico with some Harvard friends. I told Mary Anne before I left that I planned to get a job with a newspaper there and forgo college for a year. I liked the way this sounded. I could imagine the young Hemingway doing something similar. I asked Mr. Fitzgerald to write a letter of recommendation that I could carry with me. "Mr. Kidder is competent to report on a variety of subjects," it read. But I didn't know anyone in Mexico. My Spanish didn't work as well there as it had in classrooms at Andover. I wouldn't have known even how to ask for a job. I came back embarrassed, but to my relief Mary Anne didn't seem surprised. "I guess you were worried about the draft," she said.

In fact, I hadn't thought about the draft. And I didn't think about it again for months. Gradually, though, as junior year wore on, I began to worry in a more general way. I would graduate in only a little more than a year. What would I do then? What was I **supposed** to do?

At the A.D. Club, a visiting graduate member had told us, "We like to think that we do not forget our young graduates, when they begin their business careers." The promise of a future that I didn't want but could always fall back on gave me a certain comfort when I was inside the clubhouse. A steward, cook, and waiter served hot, savory lunches to undergraduate members in a dark, medieval-looking room with leaded glass windows, around a great table, elegant and heavy, solid as a Boston fortune dating from the China trade. After lunch one afternoon in the early spring of 1966, I sat down in a leather armchair at the front of the building, beside windows that looked out over Massachusetts Avenue and across it toward Harvard Yard. I liked to sit there. It was like the view from the windows of a train rolling through a city, a glimpse of other lives from a comfortable seat. My friend Jock sat in a leather chair, facing me.

He always wore beautiful clothes and seemed perfectly at ease in them; whereas even that hand-made suit I'd bought didn't seem to fit me right. Jock was one of those people who seem genuinely friendly around everyone, and curious about everyone, too. I asked him what he planned for the year after next, after graduation.

He smiled, a slightly mischievous smile, a little like Mary Anne's. He sang a snatch of the old tune "I'm in the Army Now."

"You **joined** the Army?"

He uncrossed his legs and leaned toward me. "They have a brand-new, one-year ROTC program. You go to basic training this summer and the summer after graduation. You take ROTC courses senior year, and . . ." He smiled. "That's all! They make you an officer. You have to go in the service anyway. Who wouldn't rather be an officer?"

Then one of my roommates told me he, too,

was joining up. So were others from the clubs. I had no better plan. My father would approve. I hadn't read the great antiromantic books of World War I, **All Quiet on the Western Front, Goodbye to All That.** I doubt they would have made as much sense to me as Hemingway's **A Farewell to Arms.** Hemingway himself had volunteered.

OUT THE WINDOWS OF THE ARMY BUS THAT TOOK us from the airport to Fort Knox, the landscape suddenly became geometrical. I saw a land of straight, paved streets and rectangular, yellow buildings; paths bordered by round stones painted white; and perfect rows of boys in olive drab jogging down the sidewalks. A man in a wide-brimmed Smokey Bear hat met us at the bus's door, and in a moment he was bellowing, almost in a marching cadence. "If you **cadets** can't get your heads outa your assholes! Reach down and grab your ears! And see if you can't pull them out! Far enough to hear me! **Get** in a **fucking** line!"

There were times during those eight weeks when I'd be marching in the ranks and feel swept up. The voice of the drill instructor, six-foot-six-inch Sergeant Fisher, calling, "You had a good home but you **left**." My voice and all the others responding, "You're **right**!" I felt vigorous, the vigor of a healthy young animal outdoors. A purely physical pleasure; if you thought about it, you'd spoil it. It was like the thrill one can feel in churches when all voices are lifted—the sound of the cadence, two dozen pairs of boots all hitting pavement at once. And there was this feeling: we are formidable, **we**. I didn't care for much of the rest of basic training, though. For the shaved-to-the-scalp haircuts and group punishments that made all of us the same. The assignment of KP and other unpleasant chores according to the location of your surname in the alphabet, which gave the W's and Z's a slight, unfair advantage. Mornings in formation in front of mustard-colored barracks, the drill instructor bellowing in my face, "I didn't ask you fo' no weather report, cah-det. Gimme twenty-five!" When all I'd said was "Good morning, Sergeant Fisher."

I regretted having joined the Army then, and also in the fall of 1966, when I came back to Harvard, with my shaved head still recovering. No one in Cambridge could have ignored the existence of the war in Vietnam that fall. Once a week we ROTC students had to put on dress-green uniforms and bus driver–type hats with little brass eagles on them, and walk across the campus to the ROTC building. Occasionally, other students would knock off cadets' hats or call us baby killers. So far I'd avoided confrontations by hitching rides with Jock, who had a car. Then one day I couldn't find him. I left my room in uniform alone and took a side street, skirting Harvard Yard, the brim of my hat pulled down so that I couldn't see the faces of people I was passing, and so that they, I hoped, could not see mine. Once a pair of legs stopped in front of me, but I walked quickly around them. I never missed my ride again.

Sometime that year I heard that several ROTC cadets from my class had gotten discharged by feigning mental illnesses. But I couldn't imagine getting away with that, and I didn't dare quit outright. Someone told me that you lost your student deferment if you did.

FOR THREE YEARS I'D GONE OUT WITH OTHER girls, wishing each was Mary Anne, but now, at the start of senior year, she became my steady girlfriend. In the years since then I have met people who possess convictions impervious to any assault, and the way I understand this is by recalling the way I felt about her. I didn't notice what clothes she wore. Whatever they were, they were perfect, because she was wearing them. I had never liked being teased, but from her any form of attention was thrilling. I spent at least a week of senior year visiting antique jewelry stores in Boston, looking for a golden comb that she might wear in her hair. The dealers didn't know what I was talking about, and neither did I. Did I mean a tiara? No, that didn't sound right.

She had, I suppose, all the physical qualities that women claim for themselves in personal ads nowadays—slim, curvaceous, athletic. But I hardly noticed her separate qualities. When we were apart, I could hear her voice anytime I tried—often laughing, often slightly mocking, calling me Tray-Tray, or "my master," answering boastfulness and pretension with "bi-ig man," and "touch you," and when I'd ask if she'd go somewhere with me, "Maybe I will, and then again . . . ," with her eyebrows lifting. At any moment, I felt, she might skip away, waving over her shoulder. I made her stand for so much else besides herself, for childhood and the seacoast and my sense of glorious, unnamed purpose, that I wonder if I ever saw her as she really was, and not just as an idea of mine, like that perfect story I dreamed of possessing.

I couldn't stop thinking about the other men who might be in her life, and the ones she might be about to meet. I was so afraid of saying the wrong thing in her presence, and then of having just said the wrong thing, that I rarely stopped talking. When she got a chance to speak, I was usually busy planning my next attempt to be impressive, so I rarely listened carefully. In retrospect, her patience seems amazing. It did have limits, though.

One evening she was supposed to meet me at my room in Adams House. She came early. When I arrived, she'd already read the latest entries in the journal I'd been keeping. It contained the beginnings of several aborted short stories, but also, lately, descriptions of the way I would feel if I lost her—"the loneliness, like a light vapor winding around me inside"—and the desperate acts I'd commit—shoot myself in the woods beside my childhood home, drive off a bridge, volunteer for combat in Vietnam.

Actually, I had left the journal in plain sight. I knew she was interested in my writing; she always encouraged me. I thought for a moment of feigning outrage that she'd invaded my privacy, but in fact I was delighted that she had. I just wished her eyes had fallen on different passages.

"You want me to feel sorry for you," she said.

Of course I did, but that wasn't half of what I wanted her to feel. "No! That was fiction," I said.

She wasn't buying that, of course. Later that night I looked through the journal. At the end of one of my unfinished stories, she had written, "Blah!"

I graduated from Harvard and went through eight more weeks of basic training at Fort Devens, an hour west of Boston. Mary Anne came to the commissioning ceremony, which wasn't much, just another parade. I put the second lieutenant's gold bar on my collar, and once we'd driven a few miles from the post, I asked her to pull over. I took off my uniform shirt and put on a civilian one. "Poor Tray-Tray," Mary Anne said, but without irony this time.

A few months later, we broke up. Mary Anne said she was in love with someone else. I'd written my honors thesis on F. Scott Fitzgerald. Studying **The Great Gatsby,** I had at times imagined myself in the title role. I suppose I could have rehearsed the scene in which Gatsby acknowledges that the woman he loves obsessively might once have loved another man, then quoted him to myself and said, "In any case, it was just personal." But books could transport me only so far. My world turned olive drab in feeling, and then it did in fact.

BRAVE LIEUTENANTS

THE ARMY HAD ALLOWED US ROTC CADETS to choose our branch of service, and I had picked Intelligence, because it sounded interesting. A new Army intelligence officer got trained as an infantry officer first, on the theory that he should know what intelligence was for. So I was ordered to Fort Benning, the huge home of the Infantry, encircled with car lots selling fast Pontiacs on the installment plan to young men made reckless by orders for Vietnam. Paratroopers were trained there. Groups of soldiers trotted by in formation, singing,

I wanna be an airborne ranger.
I wanna live a life of danger.
I wanna go to Vietnam.
I wanna kill some Vietcong.

The war began to seem nearby at Fort Benning. It was prefigured in the person of the pleasant young life insurance salesman who visited our motel-like officers' barracks, it was celebrated in some of the country-and-western songs that popped up from all over my clock radio's dial, and it was freshly recollected and its dangers and thrills exaggerated by our instructors and by the several former infantry sergeants who had received battlefield commissions in Vietnam and were being put through the Officer Basic Course along with us rookies. We learned about muzzle velocities and killing radiuses and plastic explosives. "You tie a cord of this nice shit around Charlie's neck and walk along behind him with a detonator, and I guar-**untee** he ain't gonna **lose his head** and run." In our war games, we brought smoke on Charlie and ruined Charlie's whole day, and we learned how Charlie would get us if we were careless and wandered into a dreaded L-shaped ambush or a thin trip wire. Sardonically smiling veterans sang us this lullaby, to the tune of the pop song "Poison Ivy":

At night when you're sleepin'
Charlie Cong comes a-creepin'
All arow-ow-ow-ow-a-ound.

A captain instructing us, just back from the war, got angry at some of the class because they'd given up during the escape-and-evasion exercise. He snarled, "I'd shoot some of you dickheads if I had you in my company in Nam." I was glad I belonged to Intelligence. About a third of us were intelligence officers with reasonable chances of stateside assignments, and the rest were infantry, virtually all of whom could expect orders for combat. The two groups mixed but in general felt scornful of each other. The Infantry's crest was a bayonet over the motto "Follow Me." One young intelligence officer affixed to his door a picture of a broken bayonet and the words "Follow Him." The infantry colonel in charge tore it down in a rage and punished the joker.

Our class contained about two hundred second lieutenants. We had no enlisted troops to practice on, so we took turns commanding one another, lieutenants marching other lieutenants, usually out of step, especially if an intelligence officer called the cadence. We marched down the streets of Fort Benning past the post stockade. A taunting voice made me look to the side. A young prisoner-soldier, an enlisted man no doubt, was laughing at us from behind a chain-link fence. We passed right next to him, a young man in a white T-shirt slapping the fence and glaring while he laughed. When I glanced back moments later, from inside the formation, he had laced his fingers through the links in the fence and was shaking the tall metal barrier that separated him from us. His mouth was opened, his teeth bared. What was coming out looked like a red-faced scream, but all I could hear at that distance were the sounds of boots on pavement and lieutenants barking commands. If you looked, you had the impression he was screaming just at you. So if you looked, you quickly looked away.

One afternoon while I was standing outside a classroom in a little circle of intelligence lieutenants, something slammed into my shoulder, hard enough to knock me back a step. I turned and saw an infantry lieutenant with close-cropped sandy hair and wide shoulders sauntering away. He knocked into me that way at least twice, and once, when it was my turn to play lieutenant, he yelled at me from across twenty yards of parade field from his place in formation, saying, "You fucking dud!" I pretended to ignore him. I didn't feel like fighting him. I didn't feel angry. I'd never spoken to him. I didn't know what I'd done to provoke him. He was like the weather, like the

Army, like the war, like the wild prisoner behind the fence, part of the collective, impersonal forces of a world I'd blundered into.

Toward the end of the course we had a live-fire exercise, a mock battle with live ammunition. By lot, I became platoon leader for a day. I gathered the men (all fellow lieutenants), reviewed the plan of attack (a standard fire-and-maneuver), and warned them to be careful not to shoot one another. This was a real possibility, and I was very nervous, until the exercise began and bullets started flying. Then a peaceful feeling flooded me, memorable because so rare. The battle came off perfectly. Without a live enemy, granted. But I remember thinking, as I stood on a hilltop with my radioman and calmly directed my squad leaders, that maybe I could have done this after all.

Several of us intelligence officers celebrated with gin fizzes around dawn, before formation, the morning after our orders came. I would serve the balance of my enlistment on the other side of the world from Vietnam, at a place called Arlington Hall, in Virginia. First, the Army ordered me back to Massachusetts, to Fort Devens and ASA (Army Security Agency) school, where I would study basic communications intelligence. But my top-secret crypto security clearance hadn't arrived, and the class wouldn't start for several weeks, so I was given a clerical job at the post's ASA headquarters.

Fort Devens was situated in a region of remnants, of Massachusetts farmland that had gone back to forest and of towns that the Industrial Revolution had built and long since left behind. Compared to Fort Benning, it was sedate. It contained the usual rows of enlisted barracks and whitewashed rocks but also sections where neatly trimmed lawns surrounded stolid-looking, slightly run-down buildings made of brick. I felt at times as if I'd gone back to boarding school.

I'd made friends with a young English professor at Harvard named David Riggs, who had led me through Joyce and the English Romantic poets. Through my parents I'd also met the writer Sam Toperoff, who lived on Long Island. Both David and Sam loathed the Vietnam War, and Sam was writing articles and giving speeches against it. They knew much more than I did, and I'd listened to their arguments. The war was unnecessary, futile, and racist. Here we were, the world's greatest superpower, intervening in a civil war thousands of miles away, setting up corrupt governments, trying to bomb a long-suffering people into submission, all in the name of a ridiculous idea, the domino theory. By the time I had been joined to the Army on active duty, I felt

I'd also joined David and Sam's side. It was an easy conversion, really no conversion at all. I hadn't felt strongly about the war before, and it wasn't exactly the war I felt strongly about now. Vietnam was far away. I wouldn't be going there. I felt as if I'd made a social blunder and now languished in a place where I didn't belong, wearing clothes that didn't represent me. I drifted around Fort Devens among uniformed strangers, waiting for my security clearance, talking about nothing that seemed important, afraid to give myself away.

My temporary commander, a colonel at headquarters, took a shine to me. He was a tall man with remarkably white skin, not pink but powder white. He seemed slightly feminine and kindly. About two weeks after I arrived, he called me into his office and said, "My wife and I were wondering if you'd like to come to dinner, Lieutenant Kidder. We'd like you to meet our daughter."

My drill instructor, Sergeant Fisher, hadn't covered this contingency. Suppose you didn't like your commanding officer's daughter, and she liked you? I declined the invitation. "Thank you, sir. Thank you very much. But, sir, I have a fiancée."

The weekend loomed. On Friday night I went to the Officers Club. Only older men were there, all hollering and laughing. I sat at the end of the bar and watched TV. I spent most of the next two days in my room at the Bachelors Officers Quarters, gazing out the window. Now and then some troops marched by. On Sunday I called David Riggs and asked if I could spend the next weekend with him and his wife, Susan, in their apartment at Adams House, my old Harvard home.

Looking back, I know that Cambridge had begun to change while I was a student there, searching for golden combs and writing stories with characters who spoke like Hemingway's. But while I remember a student saying he'd just smoked marijuana, I also remember not having any idea what that would be like. I'd been away only a year, but the city I drove into now seemed utterly transformed, both more frivolous and more serious. Old hierarchies were teetering. One elderly professor, I was told, had made up jingles to teach his students chemistry. Meanwhile, the students were rallying on the steps of Widener Library, their leaders denouncing ROTC through bullhorns, denouncing the war, denouncing all authority. Parietal hours were about to be swept away. Posters read, "Make love not war." In Harvard Square, men wore beards and ponytails. I glanced at my reflection in the windows of the Harvard Coop. My hair was barely long enough to part. I wandered down to the Charles. It was springtime. Couples lay on the grassy banks. Girls wore thin Mexican blouses, the sort with drawstrings at the neck. I coveted every pair of lolling breasts.

I had separated myself from my social class, from my student generation. Now I found myself looking in from the outside at my old life, and everyone there, on the other side, seemed to be having a great time, while opposing the war—**by** opposing the war. Didn't something like this happen in **Lysistrata,** the ancient antiwar play, which I'd read in boarding school? India-print skirts went swishing by, short as tennis dresses. To me, they seemed like invitations. I thought I'd gladly trade my uniform for sex. I ran into a friend at the Casablanca ("the Casa B"). I followed him to a party. He introduced me to the host, who looked at my cropped hair and wouldn't shake my hand. I put my hand back in my pocket and smiled manfully. But others there were more forgiving. I sat on a cushion on the floor. A pipe was being passed around the room. It came to me. "Here you go, man." I drove back to Fort Devens late that night, imagining that the MP at the gate would arrest me for red eyes. But my parking sticker identified me as an officer, and he saluted crisply, then waved me on, back inside the Army.

Classes began. My training went indoors. At moments I almost missed Fort Benning's thumping boots, its smells of canvas and cordite. It was hard to stay awake in the classrooms, though learning how to break the code of a make-believe message was entertaining, like a party game.

Robert McNamara, the secretary of defense, called the Army the "largest single educational complex" in the history of the world. Maybe he believed this, but he said it in order to justify lowering the "intelligence standards" for admission to the Army. He said he wanted to give underprivileged, undereducated boys a chance to learn marketable skills. The actual effect, of course, was to keep children of the wealthier classes out of the draft and safely in college, while the lower-class, "marginally qualified" draftees went on to learn how to fire machine guns and mortars. To me, the Army seemed like the world's largest factory, because of the interchangeability of its human parts. ASA school was like a college with a curriculum designed so that virtually anyone could teach it. After classes, Friday afternoon, I hurried back to Cambridge.

Saturday morning I took a stroll with Susan Riggs. A tall blond woman waved to her. "Oh, look, it's Joanie," Susan said, waving back. Susan introduced us. We shook hands. Joanie's hands felt not limp but very gentle. She had fragile-looking wrists. I liked her simple ponytail. The miniskirt she wore wasn't right for her. It made her thighs look heavy. I didn't mind. I glanced away, determined not to stare, and when I turned back, I saw that she was biting her lip, looking me up and down.

"You look like Hamlet," she said. She made a little laugh, almost a giggle. And then, turning her face slightly away, she said, "I bet you have a lot of girlfriends."

"No, not really," I said.

Joanie had a peaceful, quiet, wistful quality, and a cooing voice, but she was very direct. We had our first date at her apartment, not far from Harvard Yard. Her rooms were full of batik fabrics and hempy things, and they had a sweet smell, a mixture of dried eucalyptus and, faintly, marijuana smoke. This was the place I regretted losing to the Army. She said I could stay there for the weekend, but we couldn't make love until the following one. So much for the wrestling matches on couches in undergraduate rooms. She was several years older. She seemed like a grown-up, like an experience I was supposed to have and almost hadn't, and I was missing her already—her cooing voice, her graceful hands, her ponytail—and regretting the moment when I would go away for good. She asked nothing of me, though sometimes she'd say she wished I'd act less boyishly.

I drove back to Fort Devens very early Monday morning. In the classrooms, the instructors droned on about ciphers and codes and communications networks. I closed my eyes, remembering the scent of Joanie's apartment. I opened my eyes and looked around and saw a room with gray steel desks and young officers with crew cuts, taking notes about the constituent parts of the "intelligence community." I liked many of these guys, these fellow lieutenants, but I wasn't like them, I thought. They didn't seem to mind being numerals in the Army's vast tables of organization and equipment. Maybe they just didn't realize that the Army could assert its rights of ownership in all of us, at any time, in almost any way it wanted. I had escaped the worst. In a couple of months I'd go to Arlington Hall. I would spend the two years of my enlistment in the States, keep my mouth shut, get an honorable discharge, and never look back. Meanwhile, this Friday night, I'd go to Joanie's pad.

I doodled in my notebook. Two years, I thought. That seemed like an entire future. I hadn't even talked to Mary Anne for months but was still seeing myself through her eyes. Wouldn't my plan seem too tame to her? Would I seem too timid? I wouldn't have minded something dramatic happening to me, as long as the local authorities didn't take away next weekend's pass and keep me from going to Joanie's. They did that now and then, I knew, when for instance they needed some lieutenants to march troops in a parade.

I walked toward my next class down a hallway through an administrative building, along a worn but shiny floor. No doubt some private was forced to wax and buff it every night. A captain coming the other way, someone I had never met, peered at my name tag. I glanced at him and walked past. "Kidder," he called to my back. "You're going to Vietnam."

"No," I told him, turning around. "No, I'm going to Arlington Hall."

"You're going to Vietnam, Lieutenant. I just got your orders today."

"You're kidding!" I said.

He drew back and stared at me. I have a clear but impossible recollection of myself standing there in my green Army suit, brass buttons and insignia, shiny black low-quarter shoes, with my mouth wide open and my eyes grown enormous behind my glasses. I remember feeling scared all at once that this captain could see into my mind. "Oh, okay, sir. That's great, sir." And he walked away, looking back at me once.

In my class there was an odd, birdlike lieutenant. I don't remember his name. He looked like an intellectual but didn't seem very smart. Then again, I'd decided that no one my age who had joined the Army could be very smart. When he heard about my reassignment, he took me aside and said indignantly that the Army shouldn't send me to Vietnam; they had no business wasting educations like mine. My opinion of him rose immediately. I hadn't thought of that, but obviously he was right. He said I should call the colonel I had worked for. He told me the colonel would feel outraged, too, and would probably get my orders changed. I called him from my room at the BOQ. Maybe I should have gone to dinner with his daughter after all.

I said I thought the Pentagon might have made a mistake, and if so, perhaps he could rectify it.

It must have been an astonishing phone call for him, but he replied calmly. He didn't think he could do anything about my orders. "And I wouldn't even if I could, Lieutenant Kidder." He added, "I'd be clicking my heels with joy if I were you."

I backed right off. "Oh, well, in that case, sir, I **am** glad I'm going. I was just wondering, sir, and thanks a lot for setting me straight."

I had decided that everyone who fled to Canada, and better yet burned his draft card, had pure motives. I believed in Muhammad Ali's sacrificing his championship to refuse induction ("Ain't no Vietcong never called me nigger," he'd said, supposedly.) For a month or so, I'd heard rumors about a young officer right here at Fort Devens who had committed his own dramatic act of conscience and disobeyed orders for Vietnam. I knew the story must be true, because his name had come up in class not long ago, and our instructor, a field grade officer, had said, "Well, the guy's got a pair, I'll give him that." I made a few discreet inquiries. The outlaw's name was Dennis Morrisseau. He now languished under arrest in our Bachelors Officers Quarters, just two doors down the hall from my room. And yet I'd never even seen him.

The BOQ had floors of gray linoleum tile and cement block walls painted cream. It was always very still inside. The place reminded me of one I'd visited before, maybe in my dreams, a place like a dentist's office building after hours. I made sure the hallway was empty. I had every right to visit the renegade lieutenant, but my hand trembled when I lifted it to knock on his door.

"What do you want?" said an angry-sounding voice from inside.

"I live down the hall," I answered, in a hoarse and hurried whisper to the doorjamb. I didn't want to say my name aloud. "I just want to talk."

"Yeah. Sure you do," said the voice.

I walked quickly away.

But I decided to try again a few days later, and this time he let me in. He locked his door behind us. His room was exactly like mine, except that his was lived in. He had a hot plate and a small refrigerator, which he opened, offering me a beer. We sat facing each other in Army-issue easy chairs. I made some notes of this encounter about four years after the fact. In them, I put words in his mouth that I can't now be sure were his, but I know I got the gist. "Sorry about last week," he said.

"Three days ago?" I said.

He pointed at me to indicate that I was right. "I thought you were an MP. I was thinking they were coming to haul me out of here and charge me officially. And I'm not going to let them in."

He was smaller than I had expected. He had dark hair, and he wore green dress pants and an Army-issue light brown dress shirt, which looked too small on him, especially around the waist. He must have put on weight. He huddled in his chair.

For a moment I wondered if he was lost in paranoia. But no. He told me the lieutenant who had moved in next door to him a few weeks ago seemed like a real nice guy. That lieutenant had called on him to say hello and had told him right off that he belonged to the local MI detachment. That is, this new neighbor of Morrisseau's worked in Military Intelligence, the other arm of Intelligence from mine, the arm that spied on people directly. Morrisseau told me he didn't think the MI lieutenant in the next room was spying on him, because if he were, he wouldn't have identified himself, and besides, he really did seem like a nice guy.

I asked Morrisseau for his story. It had started some months back, he said, when he'd begun speaking out against the war and suddenly got orders for Vietnam. Then he went to Washington and stood in front of the White House, in his uniform, holding a sign that said 12,000 AMERICAN CASUALTIES, WHY? He was arrested, he wasn't charged, but when he got back he was told he couldn't leave Fort Devens. He had made up his mind he wasn't going to Vietnam. He planned to go no farther than Logan Airport in Boston. His lawyer would arrange a press conference there. Morrisseau would explain his reasons for disobeying his orders, then file a form as a conscientious objector. But he never got to Boston.

On the morning of the appointed day, a colonel came for him in an Army sedan. Within minutes it was clear the driver wasn't heading for Logan.

Where were they going? Morrisseau asked. The colonel wouldn't answer. Morrisseau said, "You're taking me to Fort Devens Airfield, aren't you, sir?" The colonel answered, "Yes." Could he make a phone call? Morrisseau asked. If there was time, the colonel said. Could he file the form for conscientious objectors? If there was time, the colonel said. And then they turned a corner and through the windshield, leaning forward from the backseat, Morrisseau saw the airfield and a small, two-engine plane without military markings. The car pulled up beside it. The colonel turned to Morrisseau. "I'm giving you a direct order. You **will** get on this airplane, you **will not** get off this airplane until you arrive at Fort Jackson, South Carolina." Could he make a phone call or file his form? Morrisseau asked. There wasn't time, the colonel said.

The plan seemed obvious to Morrisseau. The post's commanding general had tainted the case against him. The Army wanted to spirit him away to another post, in the patriotic South, so that when Morrisseau refused to go to Vietnam he would do so in another military jurisdiction. Politely, he told the colonel he wouldn't board the plane. So he was arrested. Now he awaited court-martial. The case had many irregularities. He had reasons to hope he'd avoid jail but was ready for the worst.

"Weren't you scared?" I asked.

Morrisseau said, "Sure. But I don't get scared anymore. I just feel kind of cold." I think he smiled.

It wouldn't be easy refusing to go. The Army wasn't amused when lieutenants disobeyed orders for Vietnam. One of my classroom's windows at Fort Devens looked down on the fenced-in exercise grounds of the post stockade, a small asphalt playground. Recently, since I'd gotten my orders, I'd been watching a young inmate shooting baskets inside the fence, dressed in monstrous-looking boots that must have been filled with lead. He would come outside at the same time every day and play by himself in slow motion, out in the open air for about fifteen minutes. Then a tall sergeant would emerge and lead the young man back to jail. To me just now, the Army seemed to offer only various forms of imprisonment. You couldn't get away, and if you tried, the prison just got smaller.

But Morrisseau and I were drinking beer, and as the conversation wore on, I felt bolder. Several times I said, "The bastards!" Several times I told Morrisseau, "I might refuse my orders." He didn't tell me what he thought I ought to do. He just said, "I know I wouldn't let them send me over there to kill and die." He rummaged around among his piles of folders and clippings, then handed me a copy of the famous photograph that captures the Saigon chief of police in the act of executing a member of the Vietcong: the prisoner stands, hands bound behind him, his head beginning to recoil from the impact of the bullet. "Look at that. Just look at it!" said Morrisseau.

I glanced around the room: a box of cereal, a few utensils on a windowsill, a stack of law books in a corner with a baseball mitt on top of them. He'd been sequestered here for months. I wondered how he stood it. He was saying he planned to run for public office after all of this was over. He was going to get something for himself out of this. And it was as if the alcohol in me evaporated. He wasn't a saint, but he had moral courage, and he knew it. It seemed like something worth knowing.

I said we should play a game of catch outside one of these days. Oh, he said, he'd love to throw a baseball again. Promising to come by with my own fielder's mitt soon, I left his room. I felt a great deal better once I got outside. That guy in Cambridge would certainly shake my hand if he had seen me back in there. Maybe I really would refuse to go to Vietnam. Outside that room, the prospect didn't seem so scary after all.

The next evening I went to the Officers Club and sat down at the bar next to one of the lieutenants from my class. We began to talk about the Army. I said I couldn't wait to get out. "What are you going to do with the rest of your life?" I asked him.

"I'm staying in," he said. He didn't love the Army, he explained, but if you put in twenty years, you got a decent pension, and you'd be only forty-one years old.

This guy would trade twenty years of youth for a comfortable middle age. I had a familiar feeling, utterly irrational, that something would go deeply wrong if I didn't point out right away the enormous differences between us. "You know what I did yesterday?" I said. "I visited Morrisseau. He's **my** idea of a hero."

The lieutenant who was bucking for a comfortable retirement seemed suitably impressed. In fact, he looked worried. Then he said, "I'd watch out if I were you. You know the lieutenant who has the room between Morrisseau and you?"

"Yeah, I've heard about him."

"Well, he got pretty drunk in here the other night and started bragging about how he was in MI and he knew the names of everybody who had gone into Morrisseau's room. I don't know if he tapes the conversations, but I'd be careful what I said in there."

I seem to remember a slight loss of color vision, so that the barroom and the lieutenant beside me remain in my memory painted a pale blue. What had I said in Morrisseau's room?

Nothing unusual happened the next two days. I decided I had simply heard another barroom rumor. I trudged into the main classroom building. It looked like one I'd known at Andover, neo-Georgian, brick, tall-ceilinged with echoing hallways. But it had doors like smaller versions of the doors to bank vaults, with combination locks and handwheels on their faces. The armored door to my classroom was open. A sergeant with a roster stood beside it, politely asking for our names as we filed past.

"Lieutenant Kidder. I'm sorry, sir. You can't come in."

"What?"

He showed me the roster. I saw a red line slicing through my name and rank and service number.

"I'm sorry, Lieutenant. It's probably some mistake. You'll have to wait for Mr. Hatfield."

In a moment, as if on cue, a very small man, nearly a midget, came around the corner. He took the clipboard from the sergeant. He looked at the roster sheet. He looked up at me. "You better come with me, Lieutenant." He wore the gold and green bar of a warrant officer, a mysterious rank, I'd always thought. I walked beside him down the echoing hall. "Probably some clerk just had a bad day, huh?"

Mr. Hatfield looked up at me inquisitively. He didn't speak.

"You better wait out here, Lieutenant."

He disappeared with the clipboard through another safelike door. The sign above it read MI.

I waited across the hallway, beside a large, old-fashioned radiator, whose hillocks and valleys and chipped layers of paint I knew intimately by the time Mr. Hatfield reappeared, about twenty minutes later.

"This was just a mistake, Lieutenant," he said. He said the roster had been prepared some months ago, before my security clearance had arrived.

I didn't believe him, of course. I was sure he had listened to excerpts of my chat with Morrisseau and had realized I wasn't the type they needed to worry about. But what did I care about that? I could have hugged that laconic, tiny man. The heavy door swung open and let me into class, back among my peers. I became a model student all that day, and even for a few days afterward, raising my hand to ask and answer questions about direction finding and long-running polyalphabetic keys.

I used to tell this story to friends in the antiwar movement, describing my fear without its irrational components. I would say that all my courage drained out of me into that radiator while I waited in the hall. That isn't true. I retained what courage I had. On another day soon afterward, I kept my promise and played catch with the arrested lieutenant on the grass outside the BOQ.

He had to make a phone call first, for permission to go outside.

It was easily the most nerve-racking game of catch I'd ever played. I imagined the spy from Military Intelligence watching us through his blank second-story window. Just like him not to let us see him. I let the game of catch go on for a time, then purposely made a bad throw. I made it look as if the ball had slipped out of my hand. I walked over to pick it up, so that I was standing quite close to Morrisseau. Then I said, from the corner of my mouth, "That lieutenant next door to you knows everybody who comes in your room, and I think he records your conversations."

Morrisseau nodded. I moved back to my position. We tossed the ball lazily back and forth. "Thanks," he said.

I never saw him again. But I imagined him, when I went off on my thirty-day pre-Vietnam leave, and as those days dwindled: walking in front of the White House with an antiwar sign, in uniform no less; looking out the windshield of an olive-drab sedan at an unmarked airplane with its propellers spinning and its door standing open for him; waiting hour after hour, day after day, in his little room, for the knocking of the MPs. I couldn't see myself in any of those pictures. In the end, I think I went to war because it seemed like the safest thing to do.

I WENT TO OYSTER BAY TO BREAK THE NEWS TO my parents. I waited until I was alone with my father in the living room. I walked over to the hearth, and leaning an elbow on the mantelpiece I said, "Dad, I've got orders for Vietnam."

He grimaced. Then he glanced toward the

kitchen and said, "Don't tell your mother." Of course, she was upset when he told her, but she tried not to show it.

My older brother was an enlisted man in the Marines, safely stationed in Washington. When he heard the news, he offered to volunteer for Vietnam so that I wouldn't have to go. I'm not sure this was possible. But I was grateful he had made the offer. Now I could turn him down. "Thanks," I told him over the phone. "But I can't let you do that."

Some days later, back in Cambridge, I decided to write him a letter. I sat down in a window seat in an entryway in Adams House. Two floors above was the room where I had read Walter Jackson Bate's biography of John Keats. I remembered the line I liked best: ". . . and John, with perhaps the greatest poetic endowment England has witnessed since the death of Milton, died at twenty-five in Rome." I remembered the lines from Keats's last letter, to a friend: "I can scarcely bid you good bye even in a letter. I always made an awkward bow." I wrote on and on to my brother, about the Army and the unjustness of the war, about memories from childhood. Then I wrote that, if things went badly in Vietnam, there shouldn't be a fancy funeral. As for the $13,000 our grandmother had given each of us, he should divide it between himself and our younger brother. Suddenly, I felt tired

of the voice in my mind. Maybe I'd finish the letter later. By evening I'd forgotten about it.

Inevitably, I thought of Mary Anne. I wouldn't
tell her I was going to Vietnam. She'd be shocked
and sorry when, in a month or so, she heard the
news. Harvard's academic semester had ended.
The A.D. Club was mostly empty. I still had a key.
I wandered through the rooms, and every time I
passed the little one that contained the pay phone,
I felt a tingling all over. Not to make the phone
call was the noble thing to do. Even better,
though, would be to call and not to mention the
cloud that hung over me. Then, later on, she'd
realize that I had called to say goodbye.

"Mary Anne, hi. It's Tracy. I just called to tell
you I'm going to Vietnam." The last time I'd seen
her, months ago, back before Infantry School, I'd
said I might volunteer for the war. Now I said, "I
don't want to go."

"I don't want you to go either," she said.

We made a date, to have ice cream cones in
Harvard Square the next afternoon. Joanie had
planned a dinner party for that night, a special
dinner for me. Mary Anne and I walked all over
Cambridge and ended up sitting in a restaurant,
where I told her about Joanie.

"Do you love her?"

"No," I said. "I'm supposed to have dinner
with her, but I'd rather have dinner with you."

"Don't," she said. "Don't do that."

"I can't come tonight," I said to Joanie over the phone.

Joanie had a fetching way sometimes of doubling the syllables of words. "But I've been working on it all day-ay."

I'd told her about Mary Anne some time before. Now I said that I'd run into her. "And we were going to have dinner. Not a real dinner, just some sandwiches. You understand."

Joanie said, "All right. Thanks for calling." She didn't even yell at me. She was sweet. She was fascinating. She had been very kind to me. I didn't want kindness, though. I needed perfection. So I stood her up for my old, perfect love. Only she could represent the loss I was about to suffer.

It was June 1968. The year had begun with the Tet Offensive, when the Vietcong and North Vietnamese had attacked and briefly held many towns and cities, and even penetrated the American Embassy in Saigon. In the end they had been massacred, but Tet proved that Washington had lied about how well the war was going. In March, President Johnson had only narrowly won the New Hampshire primary over Eugene McCarthy, who had run against the war. Soon afterward Johnson had declared he wouldn't stand for another term. Martin Luther King, Jr., had come out against the war. In April, he'd been murdered.

But Robert Kennedy had joined the race for president. An opportunist, some people said, but I believed that he would win, and that he'd end the war. Like many Americans, I thought of him as "Bobby," and as a friend, because I needed a friend like him just now.

With a few exceptions, soldiers ordered to Vietnam had to stay there for only a year, an unusual arrangement in the annals of war. My term would begin on the twentieth of June, four months before the presidential election and seven before Bobby's inauguration. But I'd managed to convince myself that if Bobby won, the war would stop and I'd come home early. It was possible, wasn't it? Sometimes things went better in real life than in my fantasies. I'd never imagined, for instance, that being about to go to war would be so rewarding. Mary Anne was going out with me again. I no longer believed she'd ever been in love with someone else. Walking with her, I would stare sidelong at her lovely profile. I'd imagine I was trying to memorize her for my year of war to come. Once I confessed to her in consternation that here I was, twenty-three years old, and I still bit my fingernails sometimes. "I know," she said. She made a mock sigh and smiled. "It's just another one of my major disappointments." So I knew I wasn't yet quite perfect in her eyes, but I was forgiven.

Maybe Bobby would end the war for me. And I'd come back from Vietnam in seven months and marry Mary Anne. I had proposed. She hadn't agreed. I understood, but surely she could wear a ring—a family heirloom that my mother had given me after I'd slightly misrepresented the facts. We weren't formally engaged, but Mary Anne accepted the ring.

Then Bobby got murdered out in California. A few nights later I took Mary Anne to a soiree at Robert Fitzgerald's house in Cambridge. He served May wine. We sat around him, mostly former students. I wanted to know what he thought about Bobby and the war, but he said only, "This one might have helped."

A few days later a mutual friend told me, "Mary Anne feels trapped." That didn't make sense. I should not have been surprised, the trap I'd built was so transparent. But I told myself that I was the one in trouble, hemmed in by history and the Army. Anyway, Mary Anne didn't say that to me directly. She did try to give me back the ring I'd talked her into wearing. In anger, I told her she'd have to return it to my mother. But time was short. My anger passed. She kept the ring. I was booked on a night flight from Boston to San Francisco. I asked her to come to Logan Airport to see me off.

"No, please. I don't want to. Please."

I had a face for occasions like this, an innocent, wounded boy's face. I'd discovered it, not invented it, and I didn't usually plan to assume it, but I could feel it coming on and was not unaware of its usefulness. "I'd like you to come," I said.

It was much more gratifying to have someone weep over me than to do it myself. Doing it myself was unnecessary. At the airport, I rushed back from the gate to console Mary Anne, then hoisted my duffel again and set off for Southeast Asia. One of the stewardesses on the flight to San Francisco tried to chat with me. She might well have guessed where I was going. Probably she just wanted to be nice. She asked if I was staying the night in San Francisco, but I didn't take the hint, if it was a hint. Weeks later, thinking back, I'd realize she was pretty, but at the moment no one could penetrate my solemn high spirits.

PANCHO

——❚——

I HAD HOURS TO KILL IN THE SAN FRANCISCO Airport before I rode the bus to Travis Air Force Base across the bay. I wandered around the airport and finally into one of its cocktail lounges. Two years before, walking toward the Greyhound station in Boston, bound for basic training with a duffel on my shoulder, I had imagined a movie camera trained on me. I'd been aware of the camera's returning from time to time since then. Just now, it was moving in through the dim light of the lounge for a long close-up of me in my khakis, heading for a barstool. This might, after all, be the last civilian barroom I would ever visit, an idea that lent depth to the scene and didn't really trouble me. Earlier I had chatted with an Air Force man just back from Vietnam, and he had told me it wasn't very dangerous over there. "Honestly, I had a pretty good time," he'd said. The light in the lounge was tinted brown, nearly the color of my uniform. I sat down and ordered a drink.

"Hey, Lieutenant!" a voice called out.

I looked around. Several stools away, a pair of young men in civilian clothes were leaning over the bar, their faces turned toward me.

"Hey, Lieutenant," said one of them. "I'm gonna buy you a drink."

The voice had a false, harsh friendliness. They were probably antiwar people who wanted to have a little sport with a baby killer. I bent over my glass. I'd ignore them.

But then the two young men moved onto the stools next to mine. They wore summery-looking, short-sleeved oxford shirts. They looked like teenagers. They probably were. I envied them their shirts. The one who had called out, the handsomer boy, the one who did the talking, sat on the nearer stool.

"You too good to drink with us, Lieutenant?"

"No." I gave him a hard stare.

"Yeah, well, we're soldiers, too, you know. We just want to buy you a drink, Lieutenant. Okay?"

I said I was sorry. I hadn't known they were soldiers.

"You going to Nam?"

"Yeah," I said.

"We just got back from Nam. You **better** let me buy you a drink. Watch your ass over there, Lieutenant, all right?" His voice still didn't sound friendly.

I said I wasn't worried. I'd heard Nam wasn't all that dangerous.

Almost in unison, each of the young men lifted a single wooden crutch from the floor and held it up for me. I looked at the crutches, then at their faces. They were grinning at me. Then one pulled up a trouser leg, then the other did the same. It could have been a dance routine. Turning, I looked down under the edge of the bar at two identical, flesh-colored, plastic ankles. I asked what had happened. Each, the spokesman said, had lost a foot and shin in Vietnam and was going home now on his brand-new prosthesis.

They must have been doing this for hours, hanging around the bar, looking for chances to tell people who they really were, looking for a little recognition. I had my own troubles, but this didn't seem like much to ask from me.

"But how come you aren't in uniform?"

"You think the fucking government lets people on crutches go home in uniform, Lieutenant?"

The one who did the talking turned to his friend, and they shared a sardonic laugh. "You think they let wounded soldiers wear their uniforms in a place like this?" said the spokesman.

"Yeah, we might upset the civilians," said the other.

The war was wrong, but how could their story be true? Our government was misguided, but it wouldn't make wounded soldiers travel out of uniform just for public relations, would it? "That's wrong," I told them. "That's very wrong." To myself I said that none of this would happen to me. I wasn't coming back with a plastic foot.

ALONE, LIEUTENANT DEMPSEY MOVES,
a dry rangy weed with ghostlike eyes.
Alone, he stares dumbly at faces, sees
faces in uniform, of privates and
sergeants, and frankly, he is afraid. No
one ever said what getting there was
like.

Where there are tropical trees, white
sand and a giant airfield full of silver
planes and in the distance purple hills
over which the sun is hung.

The smell of Asia is creeping on the
evening air, torpid, heavy air, though
the sea is near. There are smells of
unwashed bodies in the phalanx of men

that moves disordered from the plane.
The Lieutenant's face is lost in green. . . .

The plane, a Flying Tiger Line 707, which I would later come to know generically as a Freedom Bird, was landing in Bien Hoa. That was all they told us. I assumed we'd be under fire when we hit the ground. I imagined us running across a dirt airstrip. Why didn't they issue us helmets?

It was midday when we filed out the door into Vietnam. The heat was impressive. It made me catch my breath. I walked across the asphalt runway, not knowing where I headed, in a crowd of officers and enlisted men, all dressed alike in shiny shoes and khakis and garrison caps, the kind that drill instructors liked to call "cunt caps." We passed another crowd of soldiers dressed like us. But their formation was much more neatly edged and faced the other way. As we approached, silently, they started yelling. I glanced at them, received an impression of grinning faces, and looked away. They hooted at us.

"There goes my replacement!"

"Eat your heart out, new guy!"

A voice thrown through a bullhorn, almost intimately close—but it wasn't meant for me—declared, "Flying Tiger Lines announces the immediate loading and departure of Flight"—a cheer went up behind us, drowning out the flight

number—"for Travis Air Force Base, California."
Another cheer.

No one near me in our crowd said anything.
We arrived at what might have been a picnic site,
a bunch of folding chairs arranged beneath a huge
tent roof. I sat down in the front row, looking out
at the airfield, and watched the Freedom Bird
depart. A major sitting next to me fanned himself
with his garrison cap and sighed. I sat for a long
time, wondering what would happen next. I
remember thinking, I don't know anybody here.

Soon a little group of soldiers, maybe six of
them, entered my field of vision. They looked as
though they'd been rolling in dust. They wore
camouflage bandannas and round-brimmed camouflage hats. Some wore bandoliers of glinting,
sharp-pointed bullets, strapped like crisscrossed
suspenders over their chests. They carried huge
knives in scabbards strapped to their legs and black
M-16s. One had a shotgun and another a kind of
rifle I'd never seen before, with a curved banana
clip. They sauntered by and seemed to make a
point of not noticing us. I had the feeling they
were passing in review, a symbolic changing of the
guard, though they were probably heading for one
of the helicopters across the airfield. I should
notice everything and keep a journal, I told myself,
but a voice I couldn't control kept saying, "I wish I
could go home." I didn't keep a journal.

I had imagined that the Army changed my orders and rushed me off to Vietnam to fill a vacant job. But when I reported to Personnel at ASA headquarters near Saigon, a captain behind a desk looked puzzled. "Lieutenant Kidder? We weren't expecting you."

He told me to report the next day to the office of the commander of ASA in Vietnam, of the 509th Radio Research Group, a full colonel (a "bird" or "full-bull" colonel) at precisely 0800 hours. You **will** be there on time, Lieutenant. The next morning I filed into the commander's office with half a dozen other new-guy lieutenants. The colonel had a broad face. He sat at a metal desk, a bouquet of flags behind him. He had his hair clipped to stubble and shaved to "white sidewalls" above his ears. One of the first things he told us was that some lieutenant had recently disgraced this command by losing classified information. "Gross carelessness," he called this. "You **will not** commit similar infractions." Then I heard him say, "What is your opinion of the ASA school at Fort Devens, Lieutenant Kidder?"

I was thinking about that lieutenant who had lost the classified material, wondering what the colonel was going to do to him. I tried to frame an answer. "It was very challenging, sir," I said. But I must have mumbled.

"What?" he yelled. "What did you say? Speak up!"

Before he dismissed us, he talked about facial hair. The Army high command had recently authorized mustaches, of precise measurements, not much larger than Hitler's. But in the colonel's opinion, this was a mistake. "Mustaches are dirt catchers. They're disease spreaders. I expect that officers in the five-oh-nine will **not** grow facial hair."

I didn't dare smile. I didn't feel like smiling. This seemed like a solemn occasion. I hadn't planned to grow a mustache anyway.

Back in Personnel, the captain said he'd found a job for me—to write the secret code-word history of the ASA in Vietnam. I wondered why anyone would want a history so secret it couldn't be read.

Saigon was full of tiny panhandlers. After rain showers the streets actually steamed. There was barbed-wire fencing in the sidewalk outside the St. George Hotel, where I languished in a room by myself, reading Joseph Conrad under an archaic, slowly turning ceiling fan.

But I stayed only five days in Saigon. Personnel had changed its mind. "You're going up-country, Lieutenant," I was told. I left Saigon for Tan Son Nhut airfield in the back of an Army truck, among a bunch of enlisted men. We drove down Tu Do Street past the racetrack. "Remember Tet?" one soldier said to another.

"Fuckin' A!"

Listening in, I gathered that the Vietcong had set up mortars right there on the racetrack. "Did they really?"

The soldiers looked at me. I didn't know about that? I must be cherry. I must still be pissing stateside water. I wrote to my parents:

> Riding down the streets of Saigon in an open truck in the morning's twilight was very strange, eerie. I am struck by a welter of contrasts. Good-looking, delicate little people and ruins where the bombs have fallen. Garbage and rubble in the streets, stifling heat and humidity, and then those great huge clouds billowing in from the Pacific. As if somehow there were room for awe and romance in the hovel. I'm afraid not, though. Here even murder isn't performed conscientiously.
>
> Now I am sitting in the hot, steamy waiting room of Tan Son Nhut Airbase, waiting for a plane to take me to Nha Trang. The coast! Oh, yeah. I am, as they say, going up-country. But I will stay at Nha Trang in an administrative job, or so I have been told—it pays to go to Harvard.

Boils began to sprout on my shoulders. I wrote home begging for a fan. In Nha Trang, I hooked rides in three-quarter-ton trucks to the beach. I stayed at what was called "the villa," the officers' quarters for the radio research battalion in that city. In the bar on the roof, a captain said I wasn't staying there after all. I was going up to Chu Lai and then out to one of the radio research detachments. What were they like? "The boonies," he said. I'd find out. A spec. 4 was raking the grass outside the headquarters Quonset huts in Nha Trang the next morning. Maybe he knew something. Yeah, he knew about those detachments. They went out with the grunts. Didn't I know about that? Those were the boonies, those detachments, they were the bushes. I pictured tents and jeeps and files of men moving across the dusty coastal plain, toward jungle.

I traveled north in a big-bellied, prop-driven plane, sitting in a sling chair, just waiting for the flight to end because there were no windows, and wondering if this time we would land under fire. We didn't. I climbed out onto another airfield, and a flight supervisor asked me where I was going, then pointed at a helicopter and told me to get on it. The propellers were already whacking the air, and the cabin was full except for the seat nearest the open doorway. I sat down. I couldn't find the other half of my seat belt. The chopper was lifting off, and the other half of my seat belt was missing. The chopper rose, then banked steeply to my side. I looked for something to grab on to. Out the doorway I saw the tarmac about a hundred yards below. I was going to fall out. I couldn't believe it. I was going to fall down there. I felt alone in a way I never had before. It was as if I'd just been taught another rule for Vietnam: Over here, cherry, no one gives a shit if you live or die. Suddenly, the soldier in the seat beside me (a lieutenant colonel, I'd noticed, and he looked about my father's age) put his arm around my shoulders and pulled me toward him. Of course, I felt relieved. He'd saved my life. But a moment ago I'd almost lost it. Just because of a missing seat-belt half! This was no way to travel.

The helicopter leveled off, and the colonel relaxed his grip but left his arm over my shoulders. It was comforting to feel it there. It also made me uneasy. When training camp sergeants had gotten really angry, they had called us "girls." I'd heard that if another man offered to light a West Pointer's cigarette, the West Pointer would knock away the hand, because only a woman would let a man do that for her. I didn't look at the colonel, not even to nod in thanks. I didn't dare to look at him. He might get the wrong idea about me.

I sat beside the open doorway on the brink of the sky, gazing down, the stranger's arm around my shoulder. We flew very high, much too high to throw a shadow that I could see on the land below. The noise of the engine and propellers and air rushing past made even shouted conversation impossible, and as I sat alone with my thoughts, staring down, I felt as if I were flying on my own, as I sometimes flew in dreams that I refused to believe were merely sexual, out the bedroom window and all around my old hometown. Flying, I looked down on a monochrome in green. Everywhere below was forest canopy. The whole world had turned green, every dark and brilliant shade of green. Where is this? I wondered, but I didn't worry for a while. I was sorry when the helicopter landed in Chu Lai, the gigantic base camp of the Americal Division.

I had thought going up-country meant traveling into wilderness. The base camp had paved streets. It looked like just another huge and ugly Army base, except that it was situated on the shore of the South China Sea. I spent a couple of weeks at the radio research company's compound. Enlisted men on police call groomed the premises daily, just as in basic training. Nights were hot and noisy. I lay awake listening to jets and distant big-gun fire, and wondered about my detachment. Soon, for the first time in my military career—no, for the first time in my life—I'd be giving orders. In training camp after training camp, I'd been lectured on the duties of command and been told to memorize them in this order of priority: "Mission, men, self." I would see to the mission because I had no choice, but would redeem myself in the eyes of people like my mentors Sam and David by putting my men first. Sam had written a good and moving book, called **All the Advantages,** which in part described his time in the Army as an enlisted man. I sympathized with my men already, having to call a bunch of college kids with crew cuts "sir." My men and I would respect one another.

I wrote to my mother, "We are not (I repeat) **not** going to the DMZ as I had feared for a number of weeks. Hallelujah." No one in authority had even suggested that we might be destined for the dreaded, inaptly named Demilitarized Zone, which separated North and South Vietnam. It was just a rumor I'd heard and, being new in country, believed. I wouldn't have invented a scary lie for my mother, would I? Her letters sounded worried in spite of my assurances. I wrote back:

> Dear Mom and Dad,
> One thing which I would like to set you straight about is the question of physical danger. I am always in a base camp, either division or brigade. They are literally impenetrable, and the only dan-

ger I incur is from rocket or mortar attacks, of which I have seen, or rather heard, only one. Once you hear one, no one will ever have to tell you again that it's incoming. Now everywhere I've been, there are bunkers for just this contingency. It takes a frightened man about $\frac{2}{10}$s of a second to make it in, and once there you are safe from everything, except perhaps a direct hit by one of those rockets. . . .

From the captain just then commanding the radio research company in Chu Lai, I received special orders. "Clean up that detachment, will you, Lieutenant?" he said. It was the worst detachment in the captain's command. The place was a goddamn mess, and Lieutenant Pease hadn't done a goddamn thing about it. "You need any help, you let me know," the captain said.

I HAD ALREADY BEEN ISSUED MY .45 AND OTHER battle gear. Around noon on a hot day in July, glad that I would finally have something to do, I strapped on my gun belt, donned my camouflage steel helmet and my flak jacket, tossed my electric fan, which had at last arrived from home, and my duffel into a jeep, and was driven away from Chu

Lai. We went out the base camp's main gate and turned south on Highway One, South Vietnam's and the war's main road. It ran from Saigon to Hanoi, they said. Along this stretch at least, it was two lanes wide and well-paved, a comfort to a mind looking for familiar things. On one side lay the huge Chu Lai airfield. On the other, I remember rice paddies and women with pointy-topped hats at work, a boy with a switch walking behind a pair of water buffalo, and also provisional-looking settlements, hovels made of packing crates and flimsy metal with the names of American soft drinks stamped on them. In my mind I composed fierce lines, fiercer than I felt, for a letter to Sam or David about the real Vietnam, the pastoral Vietnam that our war debased.

To my disappointment and relief, the drive was short, only ten or fifteen minutes. Just beyond the southern edge of the airfield, the jeep turned right and passed through a gate in barbed wire, a wooden arch with a sign affixed, a picture of a bayonet surrounded by flames, the emblem of the 198th Light Infantry Brigade. Spotting an officer, the black MP on guard came smartly to attention and raised his right fist. It looked like a crisply executed version of the black power salute. I wondered, Why is that permitted? I felt a momentary impulse to return it, but I replied in the usual way, my opened right hand snapping up to my right eyebrow.

Inside Landing Zone Bayonet, the streets were made of oiled dirt. The camp wasn't huge; it looked as though I could walk its barbed-wired and bunkered perimeter in about fifteen minutes. It was a patch of mostly denuded, dusty, ocher-colored ground, a fortified American shantytown. To the west, on the inland side, those thickly wooded hills hovered above us, green and forbidding. To the east, the sandy coastal plain stretched out toward the sea. The enlisted driver left me standing in the sun in the midst of my detachment.

I looked around. I was going to spend a long time in this place. If I close my eyes, I can see it now, as clearly as the bedroom of my childhood. To my right was a row of four one-story hootches, unpainted, walled with screen and plywood, roofed with corrugated metal anchored down by sandbags. In front of me was a somewhat larger wooden building, the operations hootch. A tall fence of concertina wire surrounded it, and above the doorway in the wire a sign read RESTRICTED AREA KEEP OUT. A latrine and outdoor shower lay over beyond the hootches, beside a small, steep wooded hill with antennas sprouting from the top.

There was nobody in sight. I stood beside a garbage pail overflowing with beer cans and empty C-ration containers at the near corner of a hootch. I lit a cigarette. I bit at a fingernail, that old habit flourishing again. In a moment, a young man came out of the operations building and turned toward the enlisted hootches, glancing at me. He wore a T-shirt and no helmet. It looked as though he hadn't shaved. I thought I must look preposterous to him, standing there sweating under my steel pot and flak jacket.

"Excuse me. Where can I find Lieutenant Pease?"

"I don't know. He's probably in his hootch."

The soldier didn't even call me sir.

He pointed left, downhill, at another little metal-roofed house, set apart from all the others, in a patch of weeds, the quarters of the commander of the detachment, soon to be mine. I found Lieutenant Pease inside taking a nap. He was a burly, handsome black man in his early twenties. I woke him up, but he didn't seem to mind. One was bound to feel glad at the sight of one's replacement. He told me to look around the detachment. He said I should meet the detachment's sergeant, Sergeant Spikes. But first I should take off that flak jacket.

I took off my fatigue shirt as well. I was wearing just a T-shirt when I went looking for Sergeant Spikes, so he had no way of knowing my rank. I heard voices from one of the hootches. I knocked. Through the screen door, I saw a bunch of men playing cards. One of them came to the door, beer can in hand.

"Is Sergeant Spikes around?" I asked.

"Yup," he said. "What the fuck do **you** want?"

"I'm the new lieutenant," I said.

He stood a little straighter and smiled—wryly, I thought, and this worried me. "Sorry about that, sir," he said.

LIEUTENANT PEASE KNEW HOW TO LOOK ELEGANT in uniform, an enviable knack to me. At the briefing the next morning, when Pease stood up, Colonel Mahoney, the brigade commander, the local eminence, smiled and said, "Good morning, Stan." Making just the slightest bow, Lieutenant Pease brought his heels together. He could have been a West Point cadet in his pegged fatigue pants and lustrous boots. After Pease introduced us, Colonel Mahoney said, "Sorry to see you go, Stan," and then said hello to me. The colonel didn't ask for my first name. You could see why he liked Pease. But that military bearing of his was all a front.

Pease said he already had a place in business school. I think he couldn't wait to leave the Army. Once, I began to repeat to him some of the company commander's complaints about him. His expression didn't change at all. He said something like "Let's get some of that Officers Club," as if he hadn't heard. I could imagine our company commander chewing him out, saying, "Dammit,

Pease, you get those men cleaned up." Pease would have said, "Yes, sir. Outstanding," and then done nothing at all. From him, I felt polite wariness. When I confided my views about the war, he readily agreed. Oh, yeah, it was wrong. It was a bad war. But his mind seemed to be elsewhere. He didn't talk much to the men either. And as far as I could see, he didn't do anything except deliver the colonel's morning briefing. Afterward he'd go to his hootch and relax.

A rumpled, intellectual specialist fifth class, a spec. 5 named Rosenthal, prepared the briefing for him. Spikes minded the men, more or less. The day after I arrived, Lieutenant Pease said sternly, "Sergeant Spikes, let's get this trash cleaned up." Spikes looked startled. I got the feeling that he hadn't heard an order from Pease in months. You could say my predecessor was adept at delegating authority, the only difficulty being that in departments such as group hygiene and appearance, no one at the detachment felt like accepting it, and Sergeant Spikes, I imagined, didn't see much point in enforcing policies that his lieutenant didn't care about. I don't think Pease cared about anything by now except getting out of there.

He showed me around the base camp, introduced me to my men and to Colonel Mahoney's staff, took me out drinking at a nearby fighter pilots' club—where he stayed unobtrusively sober—and then, after five days, turned the detachment over to me. However, he didn't leave. He still had a week and a half in country, and that company commander back in Chu Lai, the one who had told me I needed only to ask for his help, decided to have Pease spend his last days in country with me. I began to think the commander hated Pease, maybe because he was black. All the men in the detachment were Caucasian, but they clearly liked their old lieutenant. He didn't mind if they went without haircuts or grew long, drooping Fu Manchu–style extensions to their mustaches. I didn't mind either, in theory. Why should I care if some of the men didn't shave some mornings or the jeep needed paint? I hadn't come here to harass troops. I opposed this war. But I wanted to do a good job. I didn't want to feel that I hated being a soldier only because I couldn't be a good one.

Besides, almost from the moment I took over, my superiors back at Chu Lai began making demands on me that they'd never managed to make effectively on Pease. And it didn't help having Pease languish at my detachment, a constant reminder to my men of how easygoing a lieutenant could be.

I was working in the operations hootch when I heard commotion outside. Pease had retired a few days ago—literally retired, to the hootch that we shared ("Gonna get some of that sleep") and to the pilots' bar most evenings. I came outside. A first lieutenant from company headquarters stood by the porch in front of the building. One of my men stood at attention before him, with his heels locked. "Look at your uniform, soldier! You haven't shined your boots! You haven't even shaved! When the hell did you last get a haircut?" Out in the parking area, the second lieutenant who ran the company's motor pool was snarling at Sergeant Spikes. "Look at this garbage! Look at the dirt on these vehicles! You better get your defecation together!"

I couldn't let them do this. I pretended to a stronger passion than I felt as I called the first lieutenant aside and said, holding my hands up and shaking them, as if they wanted a neck to choke, that I was in charge here, that I would have no authority over my men if he didn't leave these problems to me, and that I couldn't do anything about those problems until he got Lieutenant Pease out of there. **"You've got to get him out of here!"**

"All right," the first lieutenant said. "Just trying to help you out." He and the motor pool lieutenant rode away, back to Chu Lai.

I regretted those remarks I'd made about Lieutenant Pease. One of my men had been standing nearby and overheard, and I knew he told the others, and I knew they liked their old lieutenant's style of command too much not to tell him. And anyway, what I'd said didn't do any good. The company commander just didn't want Pease around his headquarters, I guessed, and Pease stayed on, right up until a few days before his date of estimated return from overseas, his DEROS. I pretended to be glad he was around, and he pretended to believe me. When at last I watched him swing his duffel bag into the jeep, then wave goodbye to a couple of drowsy-looking men who'd gotten up to see him off, my spirits drooped. They always did thereafter when someone departed for home and left me there. But this time I also felt nervous. Suddenly, I knew I shouldn't have been in a hurry to be alone with my men.

Rosenthal was teaching me my technical job, and I knew he liked me. But some of the others didn't like him. Maybe he was as lonely as I was. We had some long bull sessions late at night after preparing the colonel's briefing. Large and rather slovenly, belly folded over his belt, Rosenthal would stroke his mustache and begin, "But by the same token. . . ." I pretended to listen attentively when he told me once again about dropping his Army-issue sunglasses several stories onto pavement and finding them unbroken. "You can criticize these Army glasses, Lieutenant, but I'll tell you a little story. . . ." He seemed older than I somehow, though he wasn't. But almost all my men seemed older, they'd all been in country so much longer.

I seemed to be hitting it off all right with Sergeant Spikes, too, in a more distant way. "We have to make some changes," I told him. "I'm not saying anything against Lieutenant Pease. I know you liked him and all."

"Some did," Spikes said.

I realized I'd suspected that my sergeant disliked Pease, maybe from little movements in his face when Pease had spoken to him. I was glad.

I told Spikes I wanted him to draw up duty rosters, for trash and latrines and for vehicle maintenance.

"Yessir," he said. He added, "It's a good idea."

But, I went on, he should leave Rosenthal off half the rosters.

Rosenthal himself may have suggested this. It seemed like a good idea, to give him more time to work on our primary mission.

Spikes said, "Yessir." But later on I would realize he had stared at me a moment too long when I gave this order.

That night I decided to join the rest of my men in the hootch where they did their drinking. They were laughing when I came in, and they didn't stop right away, but laughter gradually petered out. I was surrounded by bare-chested teenagers, faces reddened with sun and liquor, the sheen of sweat on everyone gleaming under a few bare lightbulbs. A couple of them were staggering drunk. I sidled up to Spikes and chatted with him for a time. I could feel the others eyeing me.

I left their hootch smiling and went down the hill to my own private hootch, in order to think. Eventually, we'd get to know one another. Tomorrow would be better. But I was having a hard time acting naturally. Everywhere I went around the detachment, I felt as if I was being studied.

There was a man the others called Pancho, and he stared at me openly, with his head cocked to one side, as if I were a curious variation of the species lieutenant. He was short and smooth-skinned and slightly round in the middle, not fat at all but round in the belly like a baby. He had jet-black hair, always longer than anyone else's. I noticed that right away, but something had kept me from mentioning haircuts to him during those first days of my command. I couldn't see his eyes because he wore sunglasses, day and night, it seemed. He'd look me over, then amble away, dragging his heels, a compact, graceful package, brushing his sleek hair off his forehead. Sometimes I'd hear him laughing softly to himself.

On a day during that first week after Pease had left, I woke up feeling tired and ornery, and then, on the way back from briefing the colonel, I noticed that the jeep was almost out of gas. The men seemed to use the thing whenever they wanted, heading off to a place they called "the ville," and it seemed to me they ought to be grateful that I let them use it, or at least considerate enough to fill up the tank. The time had come to draw some lines. When I got back to the detachment, some of them still hadn't gotten up, and a couple were wandering back from the shitter in their underwear and Ho Chi Minh sandals.

"I want some men to come with me and fuel up this jeep, goddammit," I said through the screen door of one of their hootches. Eventually, a couple of them came out and climbed aboard. They seemed sullen to me, though they may have just been sleepy. I hadn't been to the fuel depot before, but when we got there, I assumed command. The brigade's fuel was stored in huge black plastic bladders, as big around as backyard swimming pools. I saw a hose connected to one, and I grabbed it and stuck the nozzle in the jeep's fuel tank, turning back to glare at the men.

They both looked startled.

I thought, That's good. I've made my point.

"Lieutenant," one of them said. "I think you got the wrong hose. That's diesel fuel."

He got out and found the proper hose. I stood aside. "God, I hope I didn't wreck it."

The jeep sputtered a little on the way back to the detachment. A week in command and already I had wrecked the jeep. "What do you guys think? Think it'll be all right?"

"Yeah, no biggie, Lieutenant."

"Jesus," I said, when we'd dismounted. "You really think it'll be all right?"

"Don't worry about it, Lieutenant," one of them said. As he turned away I saw the flash of his teeth, a piece of a grin he hadn't meant me to see. When I passed by their hootch that night, I heard what seemed like more laughter than usual from inside.

IN **IVORY FIELDS**, LIEUTENANT DEMPSEY GETS OFF to a bad start, too. Soon after he arrives at LZ Old Smokey, he meets his platoon. The next day his company commander says to him, "Did you give your men a speech? Don't do it again, Ace. They don't need to be told what they're fighting for, Dempsey." The commander goes on, expressing sentiments I'd heard from a veteran infantry officer at Fort Benning: "Joe Bazatz came off the streets. With the lowest fucking IQ in the world. And he'll shit all over you. You know what he'll do, Dempsey? He'll shoot you in the back. You

know who I'm talking about? Your men, Ace."
Then the captain says that he's sending Dempsey
and his platoon of Joe Bazatzes out on a combat
patrol the next day.

The platoon hikes away from the base camp
into the boonies. Dempsey gets lost, through the
connivance of his platoon sergeant, the short and
stocky Sergeant Fisher. Finally, the platoon biv-
ouacs on a ridge, and the sergeant takes Dempsey
aside and gives him some remarkably bad advice:
"Lieutenant, I seen disciplined men go all to hell
and damnation without the necessary leadership.
Are you gonna kick some ass, sir?" He puts his
face close to Dempsey's. "Care about this platoon
until she hurts. Then you're doing a job." The
sergeant salutes him and says, "You're gonna be a
fine one, sir."

The men are lounging on the ridge. The
sergeant walks among them, making congenial
remarks. Then Dempsey visits them, too. But
Dempsey, "because he was ashamed of his map
work," issues unnecessary orders. "Soldier? Get
off your back. This is a perimeter. Soldier, start
cleaning that rifle now." Dempsey moves away.
While he sits alone eating his lunch of C-rations,
the men mock him behind his back. "And so
when Dempsey looked behind he found no eyes
on him, but he did not see them working on their
rifles either. And while he sat, the sun strode over

the top of the sky and took the morning away." Dempsey thinks to himself, "Everyone gets lost once, but this platoon would never get lost again. And the personnel, the men, they would come to see him the way the Sergeant had. He was just getting his feet upon the ground. When the time came, the men would come to him and thank him for making them clean their weapons. 'Saved our lives,' they'd say. He conjured up his homecoming. Walking down Anstice Street in his uniform, he could see it now. Though that was many days away, it seemed quite close, and he would not wear the medal, but . . ."

Of course, my sergeant, Sergeant Spikes, wasn't disingenuous, although he didn't always tell me everything. And among second lieutenants, getting lost in the field was a much more serious and probably more common error than putting diesel fuel in a jeep. But while our jeep ran fine the following day, that incident brought an end to the first period of my command. The men were done with waiting and watching to see what their new lieutenant was like. They'd seen enough. I found this out a couple of nights later, from Rosenthal.

We were finishing up my briefing, he and I alone, in the front room of the operations hootch. He cleared his throat. "I don't believe in talking about a fellow behind his back," he said. "There was a meeting about you last night, Lieutenant."

"About me?" I said. I shrugged. "So what did they say?"

"Pancho did most of the talking. He doesn't like the fact that I'm not on some of the duty rosters. Pancho does a lot of talking, Lieutenant. It's just big talk."

"Oh, well, let 'em talk."

I went down to my hootch, got into my cot, and tried to read. I saw myself telling Spikes to leave Rosenthal off those rosters. I sat right up, to drive that image away. I lay back with my book. An old mosquito net hung from a rafter, surrounding my cot. I stared up into its folds. Things had gone so badly already there was no point in trying to fix them now. I thought of Lieutenant Pease bitterly. He hadn't had these problems, because he hadn't even tried to do this job. A faint, dry smell, like fine dust in the nose, came from the netting. The nightly artillery barrage had begun, American mortars firing nearby at regular intervals. It sounded as if the shells flew right over the roof of my hootch. In **Heart of Darkness,** which I'd recently reread, a European ship sits off an African coast and fires its cannons randomly into the jungle. I, too, was surrounded by violent absurdity, and I was part of it. Those mortars might well be firing at targets I'd supplied to the colonel today. I didn't want to be associated with that noise, with this place, with these men who talked behind their commander's back, with this dusty hootch, the rats skittering around beneath the floor.

A mortar round went overhead. In the silence that followed, I heard a banging at my screen door. I looked up and saw Pancho saunter in. I was in my underwear. He was fully dressed, still wearing his sunglasses. "Hi," I said, brushing away the mosquito net. I swung my legs over the side of the cot. "Can I help you?"

He sat down on my footlocker and said, very calmly, "Lieutenant, you know what a lifer is? You know what a lifing, begging puke is, Lieutenant?"

"What?"

He went right on. "It's a flatdick who lifes and begs and pukes all over EM scum, Lieutenant. Ain't like a man, Lieutenant."

The Army had films and pamphlets to instruct a soldier in all the activities of daily living, and I had gone to training camps for over a year and learned to avoid venereal disease and march and make my bed and fire weapons, but I had never received a single instruction in how to handle troops. I remembered how, during her first year of teaching high school, my mother would come home almost every day in tears. The Army should have sent me to an inner-city high school for six months and let me try to keep order in the cafeteria. As it was, I had an idea that being an officer, I would be obeyed. I didn't know exactly what this short kid in dark glasses was talking about, but I could tell it was impertinent and I shouldn't put up with it. I said, "Now wait a minute, Specialist."

Pancho said, "We don't like some of the things you're doing around here, Lieutenant."

"Well, that's too bad," I said.

"We can shoot you any time we want, Lieutenant," he said.

"Oh, yeah?"

"Yeah, Lieutenant. We can."

"I'll shoot you first, asshole," I said to him, but under my breath and after he'd gone and I was sitting on my cot under a bare lightbulb, staring out toward the dark. The light reached only a few yards beyond my rusty screen walls. I couldn't see out, but anyone could stand in the patch of tall grass near my hootch and see my lighted silhouette.

GETTING HIT

—||—

MY SCREEN DOOR RATTLED AND THE voice of the commo op on the grave-yard shift called in, "Five o'clock, Lieutenant."

In the half dark, I stumbled through the weeds to my piss tube, a metal pipe inserted in the ground, then trudged up a little barren hill, like a vacant lot between two tenements, to the front stoop of the operations hootch. It had a shaky-legged table at one corner, facing east toward the South China Sea. I shaved there in cold water that I poured from a jerrican, mirror laid flat on the table, gray sky growing turquoise around my face in the mirror. In other outfits in the base camp, early-rising men were pouring diesel fuel onto the shit in latrines and setting the concoctions on fire. The scent came by on the morning wind. When I put my glasses back on and I looked up, across Highway One and the sandy coastal plain, the sun was imminent, a dawn like I'd never seen before—like a lacquered Chinese box, orange and yellow on smoky black, rising out of the sea.

If you have a bad feeling inside you, beautiful scenery often makes it worse. Even now, thirty-seven years later, tropical mornings are polluted with uneasiness for me. The commo op sat at the Teletype in a room at the rear of the building, out of sight. The rest of the men were asleep in their hootches. In the detachment I'd inherited, there was no such thing as reveille. The officer had to get up early to brief the brigade commander, while most of the enlisted men slept as late as they liked. There was some comfort for me in this arrangement. In my father's house, it was an unspoken truth that if you got up before dawn you'd already won half of your day's moral battles, and the converse also applied. Anyway, it didn't seem wise to me, just then, to try to change any local customs.

In the daylight, the men still asleep, Pancho's nighttime visit lost some of its menace. I was afraid not of what they might do to me but of what they seemed to think of me. Evidently, there was a war within a war out here, at least around my detachment, a war between enlisted men and officers. I still had no doubt that, philosophically, I should choose the side of the enlisted men. That was what my friends Sam and David, and no doubt Mary Anne, would have me do. I'm sure the choice wouldn't have seemed so clear if I'd been surrounded by other officers. As it was, I was mostly alone, one officer among a bunch of young EM who didn't like being bossed around by a lieutenant, and were no longer used to it. And I didn't like being alone—alone in their company like a ghost, or in my hootch, alone with the sound of my own mind. I'd tell Sergeant Spikes to put Rosenthal back on the duty rosters as soon as I got back from the morning briefing.

I picked up our portable map, prepared the previous night by Rosenthal, strapped on my gun belt—if you carried our information out of operations you were supposed to travel armed—and climbed into the jeep alone, propping the map on the seat beside me, a flap of brown paper marked SECRET CODEWORD covering the map.

It felt a little like escaping as I drove away in the early morning. I turned left on the oiled dirt road and drove past the compound of H-Troop, the prisoner-of-war cage, the helicopter pad, then up a hill past the tactical operations center (the TOC), past the colonel's house trailer, now lodged in a sandbagged hole in the ground. I'd overheard some grumbling about this, that the commander was displaying too much regard for his own safety.

Brigade headquarters was another plywood building on stilts, but better made than most, with a coat of gray paint that always looked fresh. It reminded me of the unadorned buildings at old-money yacht clubs on Long Island. I was nearly late. I hurried up the path, the unwieldy secret code word map in one hand, my steel pot in the other. The helmet was so heavy it gave me a headache. "Good morning, sir," I said to a major, who was walking the other way down the path.

"Here comes the spot man," he said.

I smiled.

Then he said, "Hold it, Lieutenant," and added, as if speaking to a child, "All right. Put on your helmet."

I put on my helmet.

"Now put that thing in your left hand."

I obeyed, trying to keep the morning wind from lifting the flap of paper and unveiling the secrets on the map. Even the code word written across the bottom was secret, and this major was not among the few entitled to look at it. No doubt that was the problem.

"All right, now salute me."

He returned my salute. "Now isn't that better?" he said.

"Yes, sir."

I hurried on, another day of hating the Army well under way.

The briefing started at 0600 sharp, and no one came late. All but a few who attended were officers. All of them outranked me. I sat on a bench in the back of the room with my map leaning against my knees. Now and then I listened to the briefings that preceded mine. Now and then my thoughts drifted away. Now and then I turned field grade officers around me, like that major, into barnyard animals. But I was always aware of Colonel Mahoney, seated in a canvas-backed chair up front. He was a full colonel, one step below general, a full-bull colonel. One wanted to know where he was, the way songbirds want to know the location of the local owl. This was only partly because of his status as lord and master of the place. He was short and dark-haired and the nattiest-looking man I thought I'd ever seen. On him, jungle fatigues looked like a tailored suit. He held a swagger stick in one hand, a stubby thing made of stainless steel, in fact a branding iron, with the first letter of his surname, **M**, forged in the circle of its business end.

One after the other, captains and majors walked up beside the map that stood at the front of the room and then came to the position of attention as they addressed Colonel Mahoney.

One young captain who reported on air strikes always clicked the heels of his spit-shined jungle boots. "Sir!" each would say, with the pointer stick in his hand, and then would tell the colonel what had happened in his kingdom the previous day and night, what had actually happened and also, especially in the report from Artillery, what might have happened. "And here, sir, we fired seventy-three rounds of HE Quick, results thirty-two VC KIA." I knew the terms by now. HE meant "high explosive" and Quick a fast-acting fuse; KIA stood for "killed in action"; VC I'd known all along. Every day Artillery reported dozens of rounds of high explosive and exploding white phosphorus, raining down on dots on the map, some of them dots that Rosenthal had made in grease pencil on our map, some onto spots unknown to me. How in the world could anyone know how many of the people we'd killed were Vietcong? To be fair, though, most reports sounded more honest: "One hundred fifty rounds of HE Quick here, sir. Results unknown." Which to someone back home might have seemed worse—all those shells lobbed into the countryside, all that sudden heat and shrapnel tearing through trees and hootches and people who didn't have guns.

Already I had begun to feel that indignation was of no use to anyone but me. I wasn't certain, deep down, if what I felt was even indignation. I didn't listen carefully to the briefings, but I would crane my neck to see how the colonel was responding. Flashes of his branding iron in the briefing room, well lighted now by the morning sun. A tap on the knee to the report of a firefight there on the map, of an air strike here. A slap into his open palm at the news of a cavalry assault. Sixty enemy troops mowed down in a rice paddy by the tanks and APCs of the First of the First. I had a view of Colonel Mahoney's broad face as he turned to smile at his operations officer, his S-3. His voice rang out, "The First of the First. They kill VC." Out in the audience, smiling faces turned to others. Was I smiling, too?

This all seemed like a board game. I would sit there, thinking: I don't care about this, they all assume that I'm like them, if they only knew. But I always felt relieved when the colonel was happy, because his mood dictated the mood of the room. He grew emotional at reports of the brigade's own losses. Although I knew it wasn't fair of me to assume a true difference in his feelings, it looked as if his grief took two distinct forms, one for enlisted men, another for officers. News of the deaths of two of our own enlisted infantrymen— killed in action, never just KIA, the voice of the briefing officer lowered and solemn—and the branding iron fell to the colonel's leg and his head bowed and the room went so still I could hear people breathing. But at the news of the death of a certain captain, perhaps a favorite of his, he cried out, "No!" The swagger stick coming down hard on his leg, a glimpse of his face, of his small body twisting in his chair, and a longer silence in the briefing room, during which I don't think I could even hear breathing, until at last the colonel said gruffly to the briefing officer, "All right. Get on with it."

Suppose, as was sometimes reported, a private in one of the infantry units out in the field had shot himself in the foot with his own pistol. The swagger stick slammed hard into the palm of the colonel's hand, once, twice, a third time. Cold fury, the colonel turning to one of his aides. Clearly, self-inflicted wounds for the purpose of getting out of the field would not go unpunished. I didn't hear of this often, but when I did it woke me up, and reminded me again that I never wanted to be an infantry platoon leader. The life of a grunt must be even worse than I had imagined if to get clear of it a person would aim at his own foot and pull the trigger, actually pull the trigger, and blow off his own toes. Or maybe the grunt had gotten a Dear John letter.

I hadn't gotten one of those, but every day on which I didn't get a letter of any kind, I imagined that the next day would bring the one I dreaded.

The officer briefing the colonel began to tell a

story. Stripped of its military jargon, it went like this: A platoon had entered a hootch out in some ville and found a VC soldier—had to be VC, because there was a rifle standing in a corner of the room—having sex on a bed with a woman. "Two VC KIA, sir," the briefing officer said to the colonel, ending the story. I couldn't see the colonel's face. I wasn't sure he laughed, but everyone else in the room did. Afternoon naps in my hootch and furious masturbation, as the strains of Simon and Garfunkel songs wafted through my screen walls from the tape deck of the commo op on duty: This time I knew exactly how I felt. Maybe that VC wasn't just a soldier getting his rocks off. Maybe he was in love. For a moment, I thought I knew war. And I knew whose fault it was.

I glanced at the field grade officer who was sitting beside me. He had been chewing a toothpick, eating an apple, and smoking a cigarette all at one time, an overweight man with a face like a pig's. Now he was shaking with laughter. Yes, he looked just like a pig. Maybe he'd choke on his toothpick.

When the main briefing ended, the room emptied. Only Colonel Mahoney and his S-3 and his intelligence officer, his S-2, remained. I stood at the front of the room with my map, waiting to uncover it until the screen door closed behind the last of the officers who weren't cleared to see these secrets.

"Good morning, sir."

"Good morning, Lieutenant." Colonel Mahoney leaned forward, peering at my map. I'm sure
he was fascinated by this special view, this special
intelligence view, of his area of operations, his
brigade's AO, and I sensed that he thought of me as
especially intelligent because the news I brought
him, locations of enemy radios, was so highly classified. But there was no lingering over my map,
because whatever time my briefing consumed
kept Colonel Mahoney from what everyone in the
base camp knew to be the source of his greatest
pleasure, which was flying over his infantry in his
helicopter. Later, when the rains came and he was
sometimes grounded for a day or more, I would
hear that he had temper tantrums inside the TOC,
that he'd throw chairs around the place. His tem-
perament seemed to resemble mine; he was dis-
posed to share his feelings. But the weather was
still good for helicopters, and I imagined he was
looking forward to getting airborne. I finished
showing him the previous day's locations of
enemy radios. He smiled and said, "Thank you,
Lieutenant," then hurried away.

I had one more official duty, an unpleasant
chore. For some reason, the brigade's executive
officer, the second in command, lacked a top-
secret crypto security clearance. Papers had probably been misplaced. Maybe he had a foreign-born

wife. More likely, he had chewed out the wrong clerk-typist. At any rate, he couldn't sit in on the briefing I delivered to Colonel Mahoney. So I gave the executive officer his own sanitized briefing afterward, in his office at headquarters. I'd show him the map and point at the dots on it, one after the other, saying, "And here, sir, is an enemy unit."

"Which one?" he said, smiling up at me from his chair.

"I'm sorry, sir. I'm not allowed to say."

I'd felt sorry for him two weeks before, even tempted to swear him to a personal pact of secrecy, then tell him all. But why should I trust him? Why give him special power over me? One heard many stories. I didn't believe the one some of my men told, that during the last monsoon a thirty-foot-long snake had slithered past their hootches. I didn't believe the story about the island where soldiers got sent for perpetual quarantine after they came down with incurable venereal diseases. Or the story about the ASA lieutenant who was punished for some offense by being made an infantry platoon leader. Or the story I'd heard from a black enlisted man from H-Troop, while shooting baskets with him—that he himself had done time at Long Binh Jail outside Saigon and was kept inside a steel drawer for a month. I didn't ask him what he'd done. It didn't matter, not around a corner in my mind where these things lodged, where I was like the child who, when told that witches aren't real, explains, "I know. That's why I'm afraid of them."

By now the executive officer's smiles looked suspiciously like sneers to me. He was the one who had dubbed me the "spot man." He'd get his sanitized briefing and no more from me. No way I'd take a chance on his behalf.

On the way out of the building, I passed by the open door of the personnel office and heard a loud voice saying, "I'm **tired,** man." I glanced in. A very tall black man, a private, no doubt a grunt, was leaning over the desk and speaking to a sergeant. The enormous grunt didn't look tired to me. He looked lithe and muscular. He must have been right on the edge of being too tall to be drafted. "I'm **tired** of wearin' a green suit!" he said.

I didn't hear any more. I headed back to my detachment with my map. I never saw the very tall black soldier again in the flesh, but he incubated in my memory. By the time I started my novel, he had become "the largest man in the Battalion, maybe the largest in the whole Division." A man who in sunlight "gleamed like a black jewel." In the novel, he is beautiful and frightening: "Black-fire, dark-pink coals were the lips that framed the shining teeth, they threw shape around the sounds, the wind that rushed between their parting. . . . The strength of his voice and the shine of his body and the noonday sun on his pure black skin made him: Black Gorgeous, Gift-Giver, Emperor, Warrior Prince."

I'm not entirely sure where I got the name. At a military airport somewhere, I heard a voice on the PA system calling for a soldier with the first name of Ivory. I think Fields was the surname of the man I shot baskets with, the one who told me about Long Binh Jail.

WHEN I GOT BACK TO MY DETACHMENT, I WENT looking for Spikes right away. He nodded when I told him we should put Rosenthal back on the duty rosters. For the next week or two, I kept an eye out for Pancho. But now he hardly seemed to notice me. He'd dealt with me and now had other things to do. That was how it seemed. Unlike the others, he didn't watch much TV, and he wasn't very interested in fiddling with stereo equipment. When I caught glimpses of him, he seemed to be moving around to interior music, in his gold-framed dark glasses, sometimes carrying a machete as he prowled through the little wooded hill beside the operations building. Ask him what he was doing and he'd say, "Pheebing around." Occasionally, when I joined Spikes in the drinking hootch, Pancho would arrive and, after a few beers, make a declarative statement, about "lifin' beggin' pukes."

Or he'd say, speaking of the Vietnamese in a nearby village or of a fellow enlisted man who had been acting strangely of late, "Shaky." Then he'd make a laugh that sounded like his definition of the word, genuinely mirthful and rather sinister all at once.

Around this time I wrote to Sam complaining about the Army and the way the higher-ups treated enlisted men. I, however, was getting along well with my men. "I treat my men like men."

There was an important advantage in having the ultimate judges of my performance situated back in the United States, back in the World, as my men said. I got to provide all the evidence. But a couple of weeks later an answering letter came from Sam, a consoling letter, except that he added in a postscript, "Please do not take so much pride in the fact that you treat your men like men, for they are . . . men. Indeed." The unfairness of this rankled. It's bad enough to be misunderstood when you have tried to describe something you've actually been doing. It's a lot worse to be admonished for fabricated deeds. By the time the letter arrived, though, the composition of my detachment had begun to change and Sam's letter seemed a little out of date.

More than half the men I had inherited were scheduled to leave within six weeks or so of my arrival. In the morning I'd hear them in their hootches, making the announcements.

"Short! I am fuckin' short! Eat your heart out, new guys."

Some men would spend the entire day spreading the news. If you asked them to do something, they'd say, "I'm too short for that shit." If you simply said hello, they'd say, "Five days and counting."

I'd hear this and think, Three hundred four days and counting. (Against all advice, I'd begun to cross days off my calendar and add up the ones that remained to my DEROS.) I'd feel a pang, but I wasn't sorry to see most of those disaffected old-timers leave. Certainly not the one with the master's degree and the contemptuous smile who had been in the jeep when I put diesel fuel in it. I forgot his name a few days after he left, and the names and even the faces of a couple of others almost as soon as they were gone. I had mixed feelings about one, a young Spec. 4 who, improbably enough, had come across a paperback copy of **The Brothers Karamazov** and had wrestled with it to its end. I don't think he'd finished high school, but I never met a more ardent reader. Periodically, he'd yell, "I'm not readin' this fuckin' book anymore!" and hurl it across his hootch. Half an hour later he'd be on his hands and knees reassembling the scattered pages. I hadn't read the novel myself but a year or so before had experienced Dostoyevsky's **Crime and**

Punishment—and with strong feelings, too. I thought we had a bond.

Then one night in the drinking hootch, someone was talking about the Americal Division patch, which depicted the stars of the Southern Cross, and I piped up and said that, speaking of stars, the light from many of them was so old that the stars themselves no longer existed, and that was because, in proportion to their distance from us, light didn't travel all that fast.

"It's pretty fast," the Dostoyevsky reader said.

Well, I replied, we human beings couldn't reach most parts of the universe even if we could travel at the speed of light, which we couldn't.

"Oh, yeah? Why?"

"Because mass can't travel the speed of light," I said. I hoped he wouldn't ask me to explain, since I was innocent of physics. "That's Einstein's theory of relativity," I added.

"I don't give a fuck whose theory it is!" He was practically yelling. "Maybe **you** can't go the speed of light, but don't fuckin' tell me what I can't do!"

He'd grown more and more volatile, and then rather suddenly reclusive. He seemed to avoid the other men, even his former pal Pancho. And he let the ends of his mustache grow so that they soon drooped down almost to his chin. A week or so before he left, I went on an errand to the radio research company in Chu Lai, and the first sergeant came looking for me and said he'd heard that this man of mine had grown a Fu Manchu. "Get him to trim his mustache, sir." I didn't like any of this, the fact that the first sergeant seemed to know what was going on in my detachment and especially the prospect of carrying out his order. (It was the equivalent of an order; a lieutenant outranked a first sergeant only in theory.) When I got back to LZ Bayonet, I took the young man aside and gave him this news. He made what sounded like a cry of anguish. Real anguish. Over being told to trim his mustache. And face twisted, he turned and strode away. He was the only soldier I knew who didn't at least pretend to be happy about leaving. Home meant relief to me. Didn't it mean the same to everyone? I thought he must be having trouble with a girlfriend.

He was replaced by a man from Texas, nicknamed, inevitably, Tex. At one of my training schools, I'd kept a small notebook, full of stuff about infantry tactics and the Geneva convention and, among other recorded pronouncements, this: "An officer is responsible for everything his men do or fail to do." Mainly, I'd come to think, the rule applied to lieutenants, second lieutenants especially. Being the lowest ranking of officers, they had no officers beneath them to blame. Even though I knew I was taking the injunction more literally than it was meant, when I lay in my cot alone in my hootch those first weeks, I imagined being court-martialed for crimes my men committed. More than once I thought about Tex. Never mind what he failed to do. Imagine being responsible for everything he was capable of doing.

The way I heard the story, Tex and Spikes were old friends, and Spikes had requested he be sent to us from company headquarters in Chu Lai. I think Spikes was afraid that if his buddy Tex didn't get away from there, he'd DEROS in handcuffs. I heard later, from Pancho, that Tex had been drunk even on the day he'd arrived at the detachment. Pancho and a couple of others had picked him up in Chu Lai. Tex was so drunk they were afraid he'd yell insults at the MPs at the base camp gate and get arrested. So they put him in the back of our three-quarter-ton truck, covered him with a tarp, and sat on him.

I can see him now, beneath the bare lightbulb that lit the drinking hootch, swaying like a sapling in a gentle breeze, face flushed, holding up a brown bottle of the beer my men sometimes bought in the ville. "Bom Nee Bah! This shit is beaucoup number one." He had fine hair always a little too long for inspections and florid acne around his chin that made me think, **Unbalanced meals.** In the mornings, his hands would tremble and he'd be tremendously eager to please everyone, even me—a tendency I recognized as hang-over dread. I'd seen the type he could become at stateside Army bases, the thirty-year-old private who perpetually got busted, mended his ways, earned back his former rank, then got busted again.

Tex was an E-3 at the moment. A few months before, he'd been an E-4. One of the men had told the story, Tex laughing along nervously, his eyes moving from one face to another. There had been a lieutenant at company headquarters in Chu Lai who at first had buddied up to enlisted men, even telling them to call him by his first name. Later, he'd turned into a martinet. One night, this lieu-tenant came into the tent where EM drank, and Tex, in a righteous fury—it went without saying that he was drunk—picked up his M-16, locked and loaded it, and aimed at the lieutenant. The first sergeant said in a weary voice, "Tex, put down the fucking rifle." And Tex obeyed. In the end, he was merely stripped of his rank, demoted from specialist fourth class. The Spec. 4 insignia had an eagle on it; he had to take the patch off his sleeve.

Hearing the story again upset Tex, evidently. In the dim light, he seemed to be weeping. "First Sergeant took away my bird," he blubbered. "Top took away my bird."

"War's hell, Tex," said Sergeant Spikes.

"My little brother," Tex said, still blubbering, but now in an angry voice. "Fuckin' VC killed my little brother. Fuckin' slant-eye fuckin' dinks killed my little brother!"

"Hey, bud?" said Spikes. "You shut up now, hear? You never had a little brother."

"Fuckin' dinks killed my little brother! Gonna kill those fuckin' gook VC."

I remembered times of being maudlin drunk myself. Looking at Tex at such moments was too embarrassing. I turned to Spikes. He made a face and shrugged.

Usually, Tex would wail through a collection of mucus and tears, making noises in his throat, waiting for Spikes to grab his arm and tell him to go to bed, so he could tear his arm away. This time Tex went to the screen door at the back of the hootch and yelled out, "Zips! You fuckin' zips! Gonna fuckin' kill you fuckin' zips!" The next thing I knew he had grabbed the grenade launcher and stumbled out the screen door at the back of the building.

My detachment was armed as well as an infantry squad, weapons lying around all over the place. Most men had an M-16. We had a communal M-60 machine gun and an ammo box or two of fragmentation grenades. And I had let Tex take responsibility for what seemed like the most lethal weapon of all, the grenade launcher and its various rounds, which included shells filled with white phosphorus ("Willy peter kills VC, like to ruin their whole day"). I would have had a hard time explaining my reasons to a military court. The honest answer would have been "Because he liked the weapon. I thought he'd take good care of it." Had he loaded it before he'd gone out the back screen door? Not far away in that direction was the prisoner-of-war cage, a small outdoor jail, like an enclosure at a zoo, lit up now in the night. In daylight sometimes, I'd stopped and gazed at it. Usually, an old man or woman in rags would be squatting inside behind the wire.

I froze, mouth open, looking at Spikes.

"Goddammit!" Spikes said. He ran out into the night. By the time I reached the doorway, I could see him returning, hauling Tex back like a bag of feed.

SPIKES AND PANCHO WERE FAR FROM SHORT, BUT soon the rest of the men who remembered Lieutenant Pease had departed. It was as if, one day, I looked around and they were gone. Others had replaced them. And I was no longer the new guy at the detachment.

I felt comfortable now in the drinking hootch. The weather was still hot, though with increasing rain showers. Almost every evening Spikes and I would sit together, in undershirts or bare-chested, watching **Combat!** on our old TV and drinking. Usually it was beer, which we bought on runs in the three-quarter-ton truck to the Chu Lai PX. That place was a shopping center in a combat zone, a hyperbolic extension of Napoleon's dictum that an army travels on its stomach. It was stocked with food and toiletries and cigarettes and even magazines and the latest in cameras and kitchen and stereo equipment at cut-rate prices. Often, though, the only beer available came in rusty cans without pull tabs. Invariably, we'd point this out to each other, with knowing smiles. We weren't cherry. We knew the big breweries sent us soldiers stuff that no one else would buy.

I had started calling Spikes by his first name— Stoney. He hadn't asked to do the same with me, and I hadn't made the invitation. Somewhere on the route to my detachment I'd been warned against allowing this, and now I'd also heard the story of the lieutenant whom Tex had made as if to shoot. So Spikes still called me "sir," but I liked to think that we were friends.

He had authority with the other men. He had that strong, pugnacious jaw, and he could make his displeasure felt without raising his voice, and he always seemed to know exactly what he thought. He believed in dogs. I supposed this came with having been a country boy from

Alabama. (We had a yellow dog, named Easy because she'd gotten pregnant. At some point, I recall that orders came to rid the base camp of all dogs. And Spikes said, "Anyone comes to shoot my dog, I'm gonna shoot him first." This worried me, but no one came to take her and the order seemed to fade away.)

He believed in beer, but not in drugs. (One sensed that soldiers were using drugs all around us. In a nearby village that my men called Nuc Mao, you could buy six-inch-long, machine-rolled marijuana cigarettes in cellophane-wrapped packages of twenty. "Nuc Mao one hundreds." But I don't think any of my men used drugs, not even pot. Not that they imagined Spikes would turn them in. They seemed to view him with a mixture of fear and fellow feeling that was miraculous to me. I believe they kept away from drugs simply because they knew Spikes disapproved.)

He was useful. No, essential. If something had to be done, he could get the men to do it. We had an unspoken agreement: We'd make the detachment and the men presentable when visitors were coming from higher headquarters. I didn't have to remind him to hide his pair of scuffed brown boots. He fouled up once, when a trio of sergeant majors visited from Saigon and reported back to our commanders in Chu Lai that they'd smelled beer on Spikes's breath. Both the first sergeant and my company commander confronted me with this charge. "My sergeant works hard. He's entitled to have a beer with his lunch," I said. The first sergeant repeated the charge. I repeated my defense. I was learning.

I'd even figured out a way, sometimes, to coax Pancho to the base camp's barbershop: "Look, I hate to tell you this, Pancho, but the first sergeant saw you back in Chu Lai and says you need a haircut."

"He's a flatdick. Your brother the first sergeant."

"Look, I don't care if you get a haircut. The thing is, if we don't play the game, the lifers'll be out here all the time inspecting us."

He went off muttering. "Your mother the first sergeant."

But more often than not, his hair was trimmed by the next day. It wasn't all that difficult managing Pancho, usually. There are people, of course, for whom intimidation is just a prelude, whom the smell of fear incites to further violence, but he didn't seem to be one of those. Maybe that was because he didn't find it very difficult managing me.

When I first arrived at LZ Bayonet, I'd sometimes drive with the men on their trips on the sandy side roads off Highway One. I went with them once or twice to "the ville," one of the little ramshackle settlements spawned by the war, about a ten-minute drive from LZ Bayonet, a town built largely of stuff scavenged from the huge division dump in Chu Lai. My men had discovered a couple of prostitutes in the ville. Several times we'd also driven to an unsecured stretch of beach south of the Chu Lai airfield. I remembered an abandoned church set in a field of sand so white it looked like snow, and one time when we were swimming a fighter-bomber with a wing on fire coming over us, parachutes popping, as the jet plunged into the sea. ("We better get out of here," I'd said.) But now, near the end of the second month of my command, I mostly went "outside the wire" only in the letters I wrote home.

The base camp had a Vietnamese barber who didn't speak much English, and a young Vietnamese had worked for us as a house girl until orders had come prohibiting the use of casual local workers in base camps, for the sake of improved security. Those were the only Vietnamese I knew, and I wasn't likely to meet others, now that I'd stopped going on the men's excursions. But I often wrote to my parents about two Vietnamese boys, named Go and Hanh, and described various kindnesses I performed for them. Among the moldy papers I saved, I find this passage in an unmailed letter to Mary Anne: "I am getting to be a great comfort to myself. Soon integrity will have me in her clutches. And speaking of integrity, I rescued a pathetic little whore from the ocean today. God knows what she was doing there besides drowning. . . ."

More elaborate than that, I find among my old papers a draft of a children's story, called "The Pig and the Bodhisattva." I sent the final draft to Mary Anne. I wrote the story for her, and I'm sure I led her to think that I wrote it for Go and Hanh—a thirty-page-long story to read to Vietnamese children who didn't exist and, even if they had, wouldn't have understood it.

Though I don't know why, I really wasn't afraid of getting ambushed or shot at by a sniper on trips to the ville and the beach. But I could imagine my commanders' fury if they knew I was poking around in unsecured countryside, and soon the excursions didn't seem worth the anxiety. And yet as long as they did their chores and jobs, I didn't forbid my men their day trips, even though I knew that if they got in trouble, I would get the blame. They were bored. I could sympathize. Maybe in my mind, letting them go on their adventures amounted to adventurousness. And frankly, I'm not sure what would have happened if I'd tried to stop them, since Pancho was behind most of the trips. He usually had one of the others go with him. Sometimes he went alone.

"Hey, Lieutenant, I'm taking the truck. I'm gonna go pheebe around the ville."

He didn't speak Vietnamese, but he liked to say

he could pass for someone other than an American, even for a Vietnamese, because his skin and hair were roughly the same colors as theirs. I didn't ask just how he might pull that off. Did he shed his uniform and put on black pajamas once he turned off Highway One? He didn't always say where he was going, and I never could predict, when the truck returned in a cloud of dust and I looked out through the screens at the front of the operations hootch, what new loot Pancho would be bringing back to my detachment.

One time it was an acetylene blowtorch. Another time a puppy, black and tan and cute, of course, whom he had already named Tramp. He said he'd found him tied up outside some farmer's hootch. "The zips were going to make him into soup, I think."

He didn't usually say where his prizes came from. One afternoon he climbed out of the truck with a foreign-made automatic submachine gun, bright green. It looked to me like a giant praying mantis. "What the **hell** is that?"

"It's a Swedish K, Lieutenant."

I couldn't resist. "Where'd you get it?" I asked.

He lowered his head and looked at me sidelong. "Heh, heh, heh."

A few days later, I was lying on my cot for a nap in front of the fan my mother had sent me, and I thought I heard a rustling in the grass outside my hootch, and looking out, I saw Pancho moving through the underbrush, stealthily, like a hunter, the green gun at the ready. Wherever it came from, it was contraband. Definitely unauthorized. But since it belonged to Pancho, I knew there wasn't much chance that anyone who came to inspect my detachment would find it. I had come to trust Pancho in this way. Whatever he happened to be up to, he wasn't likely to get caught. As I think of it now, this was the main reason I wasn't very nervous about his excursions. Sometimes events followed, though, and they could be worrisome.

Walking up the slope from my hootch one day after my morning nap, I saw a furtive-looking transaction in the parking area outside operations, a gray panel truck with an insignia I didn't recognize painted on the door, and an Asian man in civilian clothes handing something through the driver's window to one of my men—two flat, round, metal canisters, the kind that hold reels of movie film. I was inclined to ignore this, whatever it was, but I got the whole story that evening, when the men presented me with their plan. On one of his journeys, down by the docks in Chu Lai, Pancho had made friends with some Seabees who had introduced him to some of our South Korean allies, and Pancho started bartering with them, and it turned out they had some skin flicks they were willing to rent. Talking it over among themselves, my men figured they could set up a little movie theater in one of our empty hootches and invite the soldiers from the cavalry troop across the base camp street for double features, at three dollars a head. Actually, my men had already cleared out the hootch and hung a sheet at one end of it for a screen, and someone, probably Pancho, had borrowed a projector from somewhere. I didn't ask from where or how. It seemed better not to know.

"All right," I said. "Just be careful no one wanders into operations."

I went to the first showing and stood near the door among a shoulder-to-shoulder crowd of hooting soldiers, and, trying to seem uninterested, watched an Asian woman copulate with a dog, a purebred boxer from the look of it. At movie time the next night, I walked some distance in the moonlight down the oiled base camp street away from my detachment. The commotion at our theater still seemed very loud. We enjoyed a certain privacy inside LZ Bayonet. Our operations compound was covered with KEEP OUT signs, and as a rule the various local authorities stayed away. The next day, I reasoned with the men. We didn't want to attract the attention of someone like the local provost marshal. The men were excited, though. The theater had already grossed several hundred dollars. One more showing and we'd have enough to re-equip the drinking hootch, indeed to turn it into something that deserved to be called a club, a lounge just for us.

So they were doing this not for personal gain but for communal motives. I didn't know what regulations, if any, we were breaking, but if we were and I had to answer for it, I could say it was a project to improve morale. "Okay, one more time." I spent a nervous night, chain-smoking behind the screen walls of my hootch, watching for MPs, who didn't come, though for all I knew some might have been there as paying customers.

The next day Pancho and a couple of others took the truck to the Chu Lai PX and returned with a new TV and a full-size refrigerator, and enough beer to fill it up. And a day or two after that, Pancho went off again, and didn't return until long after dark. In the morning there was a pile of new lumber stacked in the drinking hootch, which turned into a bar and chairs. Everyone pitched in, sawing and hammering. Meanwhile, the sandbags on the roof above us, on all the roofs of our hootches, had rotted and were slowly leaking. So were the sandbags in our two bunkers, built to protect us from shelling. I'd asked Spikes to make up a roster for filling new sandbags, but the work hadn't progressed very far. It stopped altogether for work on the lounge.

The war seemed more than ever like an abstraction. I had to drive fairly often to the TOC, the tactical operations center, a building made of sandbags, half underground, to deliver information to the brigade's S-2 and to the S-3, a lieutenant colonel whom I liked. Sometimes I'd find him sitting with his feet up on his desk, making predictions about shellings. According to his theory, a full moon meant a quiet night for LZ Bayonet, and a moonless sky meant we might get attacked, by sappers or mortars or rockets. "Look out for incoming," he'd say, with a smile. So far, though, I'd heard only prodigious amounts of outgoing. Then one afternoon I heard him tell some other officers, "Tonight we **will** get hit. There's no moon tonight, and yesterday was conversion day."

The day before, simultaneously throughout Vietnam, all American-backed military payment certificates had been replaced, without warning. You weren't supposed to pay Vietnamese in military payment certificates, but most wouldn't accept anything else. So the Vietnamese people who had financial dealings in and around the base camp, and the people with whom they in turn exchanged money, all had found themselves yesterday holding worthless bills. The S-3's prediction made sense. Then again, his record hadn't been very good so far.

I didn't pass on the warning to my men. I'd forgotten about it, but around midnight, I woke up under my mosquito net thinking I was home and there was a thunderstorm, and I should close the windows.

"Lieutenant! We're getting hit!" yelled a voice through my screen wall. **"We are getting hit!"**

I hurried out, strapping on my .45 as I ran up the hill toward the nearest bunker, and scrambled beneath its sandbagged roof. There wasn't room to stand. It had an earthy smell. Was everyone inside? Was everyone all right? In the low doorway, I saw a flash of light. A loud crack followed. You could hear sand trickling onto our guns and helmets, trickling down from the rotting sandbags. Then the base camp erupted, the soldiers who protected the perimeter, who protected us, returning fire at the dark. There were shouts. Machine guns rattled. Flares were popping. The light from the flares entered the doorway. I looked around. All my men were grinning. So was I.

"That was a big fucker."

"Bet your ass."

"Lucked outta that one."

"No shit, GI."

"They like to ruined our whole evening."

After things quieted down, we came outside. We stood together. One of the men turned on his flashlight. Another started chuckling. "Lieutenant, look at yourself."

I had dressed my upper half for battle, with steel pot and flak jacket and .45, but in my haste had neglected the rest.

"You can't fight this war in your underpants, Lieutenant," said one of the men.

I laughed.

"Heh heh." That was Pancho, of course, laughing as he did when the world became interesting to him. "You're shaky, Lieutenant. Heh heh. Lieutenant Colonel Shaky."

I knew to a certainty then that, as far as Pancho was concerned, I had been accepted.

SECRET CODE WORD

——‖——

I STOOD WITH ONE OF THE NEWER GUYS, Schulzie, in the dusty, denuded field in front of operations, where we sometimes played basketball and touch football, and I pointed at the sky. Way up there, three jets, in formation like a trio of geese and minuscule at that distance, were flying right over us, heading inland. A few hours before, the S-3 had said that the brigade had access just now to the services of B-52 bombers. The planes would have flown here all the way from Okinawa, loaded with five-hundred-pound bombs. From what the S-3 had said, I thought they might be heading for locations I'd delivered to the colonel that morning.

"Those are B-fifty-twos," I said to Schulzie.

He was impressed. "Here come the judge. Huh, Lieutenant?" he said.

I smiled. I may have said "Fuckin' A" in agreement, while telling myself that I was actually disgusted by that sight of enormous military force. These days I often felt as if I were lying to all sides of myself.

About fifteen minutes later, I could have sworn I felt the ground tremble. I'd never seen the terrain out to our west, except on the map, where it was mostly whorls of densely packed contour lines, covered all over with green. But I had a picture in my mind, of bombs crashing through thick-leaved canopies, of enormous root-balls flying into the air, of giant trees splintering, while, a mountain away, a small man in a dark green uniform, a radio strapped on his back, ran on—more swiftly now, hearing the thunder behind him—along a forest path.

What I thought I knew for certain about the lands outside the base camp was that people with radios moved across them, and that some of those radios belonged to people we Americans were here to kill—to various infantry units, the most important of which was the 3d North Vietnamese Division, whose headquarters and regiments periodically sent messages to each other via encrypted Morse code. Quite often I also knew where those various enemy radios were situated.

At my higher headquarters in Chu Lai, there was a room in which enlisted men, known as "ditty-bops," sat in front of typewriters with headphones on their ears, monitoring the frequencies used by the enemy units in the American Division's area of operations. The ditty-bops transcribed the messages they overheard and sent them on to NSA in Virginia—to DIRNSA, short for Director NSA. If NSA ever broke the ciphers, I never knew about it. That would have been a secret too secret for me to know. The ditty-bops couldn't read the messages, but ASA soldiers had long since assembled a chart of the enemy communications networks, so the ditty-bops knew who was sending messages to whom when they heard the call signs of the enemy units.

Say a ditty-bop in Chu Lai heard through his headphones the commo op of the 3d Regiment of the 3d NVA Division, spelling out the 3d Regiment's call sign. The ditty-bop would at once alert another soldier, who would relay the information by secure radio to an airborne ditty-bop, aloft in an Air Force or Navy plane, a propeller-driven plane equipped with direction-finding equipment. The technicians in the plane would tune in to the signal, and the pilot would fly toward it and, in the best case, circle around it so as to catch the signal from three different directions, triangulating the location of the 3d Regiment's radio. Eventually, that location would be sent to my detachment, a packet of two letters followed by six numbers. By now I could see one of those and place it in the brigade's AO without even looking at a map.

Locations came in throughout the day, but mostly in the afternoon. I'd ferry them to the brigade's S-2 and S-3, and at night I'd often sit with Rosenthal in the operations hootch, in front of our big map of southern I Corps. It occupied an entire freestanding wall. On the acetate that covered it, Rosenthal and I kept a record in multi-colored grease pencil of the past month's move-ments of all the enemy radios of all the enemy units in southern I Corps. I can see us now, on a sultry night under bare lightbulbs, Rosenthal with his shirt off, smoking his pipe, I think, pointing at our map and saying, "And by the same token, Lieutenant, those movements could suggest a new offensive." And I in a white T-shirt, smoking a cigarette, saying, "I see what you mean, Mike. I think you may have something there."

When I was a boy, my father taught me to read nautical charts. In time, he had let me do the navi-gating on his catboat. I'd loved maps ever since. I liked to dream on them, making trips and adven-tures. And most of all I liked to use them, especially at night under the wavering glow of the cabin's kerosene lamps, when the art of transferring their symbols to the visible world of lighthouses, red-flashing bell buoys, and faintly blinking channel markers was most challenging. But to represent something is to command power over it. Maps are the tools of many ambitious people, of policy makers, commanders of armies, and youths who like to play at being one of those. And the problem is that maps are easily confused with the world.

When I'd left the United States, some people in the antiwar movement were still saying this was a war waged only between a corrupt South Vietnamese regime and valiant local insurgents. But on the part of our map that covered the brigade's AO, most of what you saw were large North Vietnamese units, and just a couple of Vietcong companies. And here was the kicker, as Rosenthal had explained: All of those units, including the two little VC companies, communicated directly with a giant corps headquarters across the border in Cambodia, which we called "MR-5," and MR-5, in turn, communicated directly with Hanoi. More than mere geography separated me from my principled antiwar friends back home. Especially from people like that guy in Cambridge who had refused to shake hands with me on account of my haircut. Arrogant bastard. He should be against this war, of course, but I'd bet he didn't know why.

For me, and I think for Rosenthal, tracking the enemy radios on our enormous map was easily the most interesting part of our lives right then. We'd talk about the locations of those radios as if gossiping about old mutual acquaintances. Their movements weren't always predictable. One night I woke up to Rosenthal's voice calling through my screen wall, "Lieutenant, something just came in you better look at. Third NVA." By the time I got up to operations, he had it marked on the map. The radio of the 3d NVA Regiment. Two days ago it had been situated many kilometers to the west of Chu Lai. Now, on the map, it sat right near the edge of the giant Americal Division base camp. I looked at the Teletype message. I plotted the location myself. Not that Rosenthal ever made a mistake. "Jesus," I said. I turned to Rosenthal and saw that both of us were trying not to smile.

We assumed that by this point in the war the enemy knew what we were up to. We imagined that their commo ops would send their messages from some empty field or hilltop, then pack up in a hurry and start running. But there was a limit to how far they could stray from their headquarters. So the location of a radio was still useful information.

The locations weren't all equal. If the direction-finding plane managed to triangulate a radio, the location was said to be "a fix," and fixes varied from "within five hundred meters," which were the best and most reliable, to "within three thousand meters." Many times subsequent five-hundred-meter fixes would show three-thousand-meter fixes to have been wrong by far more than that. And a signal caught from only two directions, "a cut," wasn't to be trusted at all.

This alarming new location for the 3d Regiment was a three-thousand-meter fix. It had been recorded near dusk yesterday. It was two o'clock in the morning now. No telling why the fix had taken so long to get to us.

For a couple of weeks Rosenthal had been speculating about the start of a new enemy offensive, like the famous Tet Offensive of the previous February. It was a prediction based on a pattern of radio activity and movement that he thought he'd discerned. We weren't trained or equipped to make that kind of analysis, and God knows we weren't authorized to confuse the colonel by sharing ideas like that. (That was the CIA's job, I'd decided mordantly, after one of the biweekly high-level crypto briefings that the colonel got from Division, where I'd heard a CIA strategic analysis that was based largely on a cut.) But there was no question about one thing. I had to wake up Colonel Mahoney. Protecting the Americal Division's base camp was his brigade's principal responsibility. For all we knew, the 3d Regiment might at that moment be about to attack Chu Lai. I called headquarters. The colonel's aide told me to come to the house trailer in fifteen minutes.

As we got the portable map ready, Rosenthal reminded me of the pattern we thought we'd seen, the suggestions of a new offensive. "Do you think you should tell the colonel?"

"Yeah, maybe," I said. "Yeah, we should! Why don't you come with me?"

He drove the jeep. I carried the map. I knocked on the door of the house trailer. Colonel Mahoney answered. His face looked a little puffy, but he was fully dressed, in pressed, tailored fatigues.

"Sir, we just got this fix for the Third NVA Regiment." I handed him the map and pointed at the location.

He sat down on the edge of his bed, the map balanced on his knees. He stared at it, and then he yelled, "Goddammit!" He looked up at me. "When was this from?"

"Seventeen hundred hours, sir. But it just came in."

He was staring hard at the map again. "Goddammit!" He slammed a fist on his mattress. "Goddammit!" He grabbed his field telephone and told his S-3, who had already been awakened, "Get over here, Nat."

Then silence inside the house trailer, the colonel staring at the map.

I cleared my throat. "Sir, while we're waiting, Specialist Rosenthal here has been noticing something I think you'd find interesting, sir, while we're waiting."

He looked up at me, dark eyebrows lowered. "I'm not **waiting,** Lieutenant. I'm **thinking.**"

There were times in the Army when the position of military attention—stiff spine, lifted chin, wide, front-facing eyes, wooden arms—seemed like the most natural of postures. "Yes, sir!"

"Is it important? Or just a **goddamn detail?**"

"Just a detail, sir."

He had gone back to staring at the map, muttering imprecations. Then the S-3 arrived, and the colonel's bedroom filled with infantry talk, names of battalions, mobile resources, punctuated now and then by oaths from the colonel. I see him, sitting there slamming his fist down on the edge of his bed, saying in a voice nearly anguished, "But the First of the Fifth is at least ten clicks away!" We stood there, forgotten, Rosenthal and I. Finally, the colonel turned to us. "Thank you, Lieutenant. You, too, Specialist."

So we never did get to tell Colonel Mahoney our theory about a new offensive. Which was just as well. A few afternoons later we received a new location for the 3d NVA Regiment, a five-hundred-meter fix, which put the regiment's radio miles away to the west of Chu Lai, where it represented no threat to the big base camp, just to the infantry platoons out there. But when I delivered this news at the morning briefing, Colonel Mahoney didn't even mention the false alarm. Not long afterward I was able to return the favor.

I hadn't paid much attention to my detachment's other mission, which was called comsec. We were supposed to monitor the brigade's radio and landline transmissions, looking for violations of communications security. Three men usually did that job, among them Pancho, who was the boss. Now and then I'd see him or one of the others sitting in operations at the comsec desk with headphones on and typing. More often, their desk was empty. But so far they seemed to be producing enough paper to satisfy our headquarters in Chu Lai. I saw no point in asking Pancho to do more. Actually, I hoped he wouldn't. A lot of people in this base camp could make our lives miserable if we caught them making comsec violations and reported them.

But Pancho liked the job well enough, the sneakiness of it. For him, I thought, this was a form of pheebing around, and he could be assiduous. There was always the chance he'd get lucky and eavesdrop on something juicy, some officer boasting about his conquest of an Army nurse or Red Cross donut dolly. Comsec guys liked to talk about those kinds of scores. And in retrospect, it seems inevitable that one day I'd walk into operations and find Pancho with the headphones on, typing furiously. He looked up at me and smiled craftily, then went back to work. A little later, while I was working on the map, he came around the corner and handed me a sheaf of paper. "You gotta see this shit, Lieutenant. It's your brother Colonel Mahoney."

The colonel, anyone could tell, was enthusiastic about his work. That day, from his helicopter, he'd gotten carried away and forgotten protocol. Not once but repeatedly, he'd radioed orders down to various of his units on the ground, saying over the air, "This is Colonel Mahoney."

There they were, recorded in black and white, gross comsec violations. Pancho planned to send the transcripts to Chu Lai. I imagined them ending up on the desk of the commanding general, I imagined the commanding general putting in a call to Colonel Mahoney, and in the aftermath, I imagined the end of our immunity from local inspections, from standing shifts all night in the bunkers on the landing zone's perimeter. It must have been class prejudice making Pancho stupid. He must have found the chance to mess with a full-bull colonel irresistible.

I said, "Don't even think about it!" I seem to recall that the other comsec guys got a little indignant in the lounge that night. "This is a war, Lieutenant." "We got a job to do, Lieutenant." Mostly, I think, they wanted to feel their job was important. I don't remember Pancho ever talking about the war, or his job, as if he believed in either one or, for that matter, disbelieved, but he wanted those transcripts sent back to headquarters. I compromised. I said I'd talk to the colonel personally the next morning.

I waited until after I'd finished my briefing. The colonel had gotten up from his chair. "Sir," I said softly. "Could I have a word with you?"

"All right. Make it quick."

The S-2 and S-3 were leaving. No one could overhear. "Uh, sir, my men picked up some radio transmissions of yours yesterday, sir. In which, sir, you identified yourself by name." I didn't dare look at his face. I stared down at the transcripts in my hands. They were opened to one example, which Pancho had circled in red pen.

Then I handed him the transcripts, talking fast as he stared at them, saying, "These are for you, sir. They're the only copies. We just want you to be aware of this. You really shouldn't do this, sir."

The surprise and consternation on his face made me think of my father, who wasn't used to making mistakes either. "You're absolutely right, Lieutenant!" He thwacked himself on the leg with his branding iron. "Goddammit!"

ROSENTHAL WAS ALREADY FAIRLY SHORT WHEN I'D arrived. After he left, I realized his importance to me, how useful he had been in keeping our little role in the war on a comfortable, theoretical plane. I missed him. Looking for new company, I'd sometimes wander over to chat with the lieutenant in charge of the POW cage. He'd been to college. There was a diffidence about him that I liked. I sensed he didn't think too highly of this war either and was just trying to get through it to his DEROS. One time, I arrived and found my friend chatting with an Englishman, a jovial, tall, broad-shouldered man with a reddish handlebar mustache, dressed in the uniform of an American Army sergeant. He was a LRRP (pronounced "lurp"), a long-range reconnaissance patrolman. I'd heard of these soldiers, of how they'd parachute alone and in pairs into the forest and sneak around trying to locate large enemy units, like the 3d NVA Regiment. It was perilous work. More than once at the colonel's briefings I heard of LRRPs being maimed or killed. Noting the man's accent, I asked him if he was an English citizen. He said he was. But what was he doing in Vietnam in the U.S. Army? I asked. He smiled. "It's the only war going, isn't it, mate?" The LRRPs had been mythical soldiers to me, and they still were after that brief encounter, like so much else about the war around me.

The lieutenant in charge of the POW cage seemed to have a better observation post on the real action than I did. He told me, for instance, that some Americans in dark glasses and civilian clothes had shown up here and asked him with voices a little too eager, "Got any prisoners for us?" They were looking for someone to torture. He knew it right away. He told this with disgust, and then one day I wandered over there and found in the room a small Vietnamese man—a new prisoner, suspected VC, my friend explained. I'd been playing in my mind the kind of speculative game I used to play with Rosenthal. I imagined myself enlarging on the little intelligence we knew and wondered aloud to the lieutenant if this prisoner might know something about the 3d NVA Regiment. My friend beckoned the prisoner over. He asked the man something in Vietnamese. Hearing the answer, not liking the answer evidently, he leaned forward in his chair and yanked the prisoner toward him. He pinned the man between his legs and lashed him across the cheeks with a shoelace three or four times. The lieutenant pursed his lips as he whipped the shoelace back and forth. Then he stopped, satisfied, like a person folding a letter. He let the prisoner go and said, "He doesn't know anything."

We chatted afterward, as if nothing had happened. I went back to my detachment feeling sick. Was there something that could have been done to stop that little cruelty, and was the problem that I couldn't do it? Forget it, I told myself. I was just the inadvertent cause of something that would have happened anyway, that probably happened all the time. Compared to other interrogations I imagined, that one wasn't harsh. The look I'd seen on the lieutenant's face lingered with me, though. How would I act in his place? As badly? Or worse?

I didn't have enough to do. I was doing my best to keep busy. I hadn't trained a replacement for Rosenthal. The map work was interesting to me. I didn't want to share it. I couldn't have begun to explain all this to anyone, that it was because I had too little to do that I sometimes had too much, and made mistakes.

On a day around this time, I was doing paperwork that I wanted to be rid of, at my desk in operations, when the commo op on duty handed me a square piece of flimsy newsprint, one-third the size of a sheet of typing paper, with the usual stuff on the top identifying our company headquarters in Chu Lai as the sender and us, the detachment, as the recipient. The commo op had routinely stamped the page SECRET SUNDAE on top and bottom in red ink, **sundae** being the code word. The content read, THE THIRD NVA REGIMENT IS ON THE MOVE.

Some brief enemy messages weren't encrypted but transmitted in an operational code, which our local experts had long since broken. These could be read at my company headquarters in Chu Lai. They were usually messages like this one, in which a unit said it was relocating. But they never said where they were going, and the S-3 didn't seem to find the information useful. I was supposed to pass it on to him right away, but it wasn't important, and I didn't want to interrupt what I was doing.

"Hey, Pancho." I'd caught a glimpse of him a moment before, pheebing around operations. "You mind taking something to the TOC?"

He didn't mind. He was far from lazy. He always took his turn with chores, burning the shit, fetching fuel, filling the shower with water. He got scowling angry if another man shirked his share of those duties, and in this way helped to make sure that others usually didn't. And he never minded errands. Anything to go somewhere. He was, I think, the most nonchalant and restless person I'd ever met. He'd told me the other day that he'd spent some time in Cambodia helping to build an ASA listening post. Cambodia, he'd said, was beaucoup number one duty, but he'd given it up and volunteered for Vietnam simply because he wanted to see what was going on here. I put the slip of paper into a file folder and handed it to him and went back to work.

He was away a long time, but that could have

meant almost anything. I had finished my paperwork and was standing on the front stoop of operations, wondering where he'd gone this time,
when the jeep pulled in and he walked in through
the gate a little more quickly than usual and said,
"Hey, Lieutenant, that flatdick message got lost."

"Sure," I said. I wasn't going to fall for that. I
wasn't easy anymore.

"No," he said. "It did."

"You're kidding."

"No, I'm **telling** you, Lieutenant. The thing
blew out of the flatdick folder." It happened near
the helicopter pad, he said. He'd jumped out and
chased the piece of paper, but a chopper was coming in for a landing. The prop wash caught the
paper. It rose, slicing back and forth, Pancho
jumping up in the air trying to catch it, and then
it must have caught a strong updraft because it
went straight up. He could still see it, he thought,
a little white wisp, floating off toward the forested
hills to the west. He climbed back in the jeep and
tried to follow it until he came to the perimeter of
the base camp and could go no farther. By then he
couldn't see it anymore.

"A whirlwind came up. It just took off like this.
Whish. So I'm out there trying to catch this thing,
and there was this guy there, the chaplain or
something. He's watching me." Pancho shook his
head in wonder. "It was high!"

"I don't **believe** it," I said. I was biting my fingernails again.

"Okay, Lieutenant. Go ask the flatdick chaplain guy." He sauntered off toward his hootch, and I noticed again how he carried himself, a graceful-looking shamble with a policeman's arms-at-the-ready air. I hated him.

Maybe it really was a joke. I had to know. I ran back inside operations, put on my shirt, then ran to the cubicle Pancho had carved out for his cot and his various acquisitions, in the front half of one of the EM hootches. "Who is this guy? Where is he?"

Pancho was lying down, taking a rest from his exertions. "I don't know. Some shaky-looking guy, said he was a chaplain or something." He described the building where the man worked.

I ran to the jeep. I found the building and the man in question, a thin, pale young soldier with a chaplain's cross on his collar. He was the chaplain's assistant, in fact. I wondered to myself if he was a conscientious objector. Certainly he seemed conscientious. He had a very soft voice. He'd been out for a walk when he saw a soldier chasing a piece of paper. He'd tried to help, but they just couldn't catch the thing. He described the ascent of the document. He said, in a tone that one might use to describe one of nature's wonders, "I never saw a piece of paper go so high."

I remembered my audience with the full-bull colonel in Saigon, the commander of Radio Research in Vietnam, and how nearly apoplectic he had seemed when he'd talked about some fool lieutenant who had lost classified information. This sort of thing reflected badly on a commander. I found Pancho in operations. "This is really serious, Pancho."

"Maybe we just shouldn't tell anybody."

I lit another cigarette, fumbling with my lighter.

"You look shaky, Lieutenant."

I stared at him. How could he be so casual about this? He should be worried sick. It seemed the least that he could do. "This is **fucking** terrible, Pancho. I'm in deep shit."

"What are they gonna do to you, Lieutenant?" he replied. "Send you to Vietnam?" And he walked away, disgusted with me, obviously.

It was what they **could** do, not what they might be likely to do. Not Long Binh Jail. Even Morrisseau was treated better than that. I hadn't killed anyone, hadn't broken the law. Maybe, as Pancho suggested, we should just keep quiet and try to forget the whole thing. But suppose by chance, just by chance, someone found that slip of paper with SECRET SUNDAE written on it along with the name of my detachment, and it was turned in. Or suppose Pancho got drunk and told the other men, who by now probably sensed that something untoward had happened, and one of those men went drinking at the EM club in Chu Lai and told the story, and some sergeant overheard and told the first sergeant, who of course would tell the captain. Then a whole skein of evil consequences was not impossible. Court-martial and a foul punishment. Pancho didn't have to worry. If we hushed this up, he'd have something over me. He'd be implicated, but I'd be the one who had told him not to talk.

I called the operations officer in Chu Lai and told him everything. He groaned. I expected recriminations, but he didn't utter any, just a long series of groans. I guess he knew what was coming for him. He'd have to spend the next week or so writing up an entire manual about how detachments must handle code-word material outside their compounds. This would mean double-wrapped packages, two couriers to carry them, and even then he'd get some blame for not having written such a manual before I let Pancho lose the message.

The news of our infraction, I knew, was moving up the line, to our next higher headquarters in Nha Trang. After my briefing the next morning, I told Colonel Mahoney what had happened.

His brow furrowed. He turned to his S-3. "Lieutenant Kidder's in some trouble, Nat." Perhaps they could spare a helicopter for an hour or so to look for the lost document. I felt a surge of hope, but when I got to the helicopter pad at the appointed time, the pilot shook his head. There was something wrong with the main rotor, he explained. "I can land this thing in a hurricane without an engine. But if the rotor's broke, it turns into a stone." At the moment, I wanted to say I'd take the chance. Obviously, though, he wouldn't. I really thought we might find that tiny slip of paper, hanging in a tree, out there in those steep, green hills. The next day it rained, and I gave up all hope and went back to imagining the very worst things that could happen.

It's a habit of mind described in a story by Borges, a habit I'd discovered on my own. If you imagine the worst, then it has already happened in a sense and seems unlikely to happen again. But there was more to this strategy, I now think. "What are they going to do to you, send you to Vietnam?" If that was all, if there was no chance they'd make me an infantry platoon leader, if the worst real possibility was that they'd relieve me of command and have me spend the rest of my year doing paperwork in Nha Trang or Saigon, then I had no reason to feel scared. But I **was** scared. So I needed to have good reasons.

My first company commander back in Chu Lai, the jaded captain, had long since departed and been replaced by a captain I liked much more. Even the enlisted men liked him. He was cheerful. He was temperate. He was probably only in his late twenties, but he seemed older. I think this was because, except for the fact that he seemed to plan to make the Army a career, he had no obvious flaws. A few days after the message flew away, he called on the landline and told me that Lieutenant Colonel Riddle, commander of the radio research battalion in Nha Trang, was coming for a visit.

"What's going to happen, sir?"

"I don't know. He's pretty upset."

"Oh, God."

But at least my captain was on my side. I was on good terms with the brigade commander, Colonel Mahoney, right? Well, my captain said, I should tell Colonel Mahoney that my battalion commander, Colonel Riddle, was coming to visit my detachment because of the lost document. And I should ask Colonel Mahoney if he'd be willing to speak to Colonel Riddle on my behalf.

"And make sure that your vehicles are washed," said my company commander. "I mean it. That's very important to Colonel Riddle."

"Riddle?" said Colonel Mahoney the next morning, seated in his canvas chair. He looked off across the briefing room, resting his chin on his branding iron. "Dean Riddle? Oh, yes." Colonel Mahoney looked at me. It was time for him to be getting on his helicopter. "You tell Colonel Riddle I expect both of you for dinner tomorrow night at the field grade officers' mess."

"Yes, sir."

Spikes had the men wash the truck and jeep and sent them back to wash them again because they hadn't done it well enough. He even worked himself, cleaning up operations. In the evening, I put on a fresh uniform and my steel pot and stood outside. When the jeeps pulled in, I spotted the one that carried our lieutenant colonel, and when he stepped out, I was right in front of him, saluting crisply.

He was a tall man. His uniform was of course impeccable, like Colonel Mahoney's, but I felt at once that there was something sloppy underneath. Maybe this impression was all in my mind, was and still is. It came from his face, especially the corners of his mouth. To me, he looked both slack and crafty, like someone with a secret vice. But after all, it was the face of a man with great power over me, and perhaps I felt revolted by the dishonest, excessive courtesy I was prepared to show him.

He was smiling faintly at me. I remember the impression. The man was going to take some pleasure in whatever it was he planned to do with me. I don't know what he had planned to say, though, because I didn't give him a chance to speak. I said, "Welcome to the detachment, Colonel Riddle, sir. Sir, the brigade commander, Colonel Robert Mahoney, told me to tell you that he expects us for dinner this evening."

"Colonel Mahoney?" he said, and his eyes widened slightly. I already knew of course that somewhere, sometime, he had served under Colonel Mahoney. Now I also knew that it had been for Lieutenant Colonel Riddle, as for many others, no doubt, an unforgettable experience.

"What time, Lieutenant?" He had a southern accent.

"Eighteen hundred hours, sir."

"What time is it now?" he snapped at one of the officers beside him.

It was 1730. I asked Colonel Riddle if he'd like to take a look at our operations hootch. He said all right. "But we don't want to be late for Colonel Mahoney now." He didn't even look at our vehicles.

Colonel Mahoney gave Lieutenant Colonel Riddle a cordial greeting at the door to the mess, though I sensed a certain reserve in him, which matched, I thought, the obsequiousness of Colonel Riddle, bending over to bring himself closer to the more exalted colonel's height, smiling eagerly every time the brigade commander opened his mouth to speak. He was like a butler, and I a butler's butler. Colonel Mahoney told us to sit beside him at the head of the table. I gave myself silent orders. Don't talk unless someone speaks to you. Call everyone sir. Watch what Colonel Mahoney does. Don't pick up your fork until he does. I had only limited experience in keeping my mouth shut. It seemed like something I should do more often. One noticed things. In the field grade officers' mess hall, there was French wine, and roast beef, and orderlies to serve them. A major seated to my left started speaking to me, and then I couldn't hear much of the two colonels' conversation, but somewhere near the end of the meal, I heard Colonel Mahoney say, "I don't want to see this young lieutenant get hurt."

"No, sir," said Colonel Riddle.

"He might want to make this his career," said Colonel Mahoney.

And I felt, desperately, for an instant, that his saying so might make it true, and that I had to set him straight. The words rushed into my mind. "No, sir, I'm getting out of the Army as soon as I can." I wiped my mouth with my napkin, real cloth. The moment passed.

The next day my company commander told me that in due course someone would come from Nha Trang to conduct an official investigation. But the outcome was already fixed, just an administrative reprimand.

Drinking in the lounge that night felt like the end of a long, hard journey. Alone in my hootch afterward, I wrote, "Dear Mom and Dad, Nothing has happened really, except that I've gotten in a pile of trouble for something one of my men lost. No cure for it, and it doesn't worry me. Let them do what they like—they can't send me to jail."

All the next day, though, I had the feeling I was being watched. In the evening, when I walked into operations, the place seemed too quiet. I sat down at my plywood desk to begin preparing the next day's briefing. The light was dim. I reached up to turn on the wall lamp that extended over the desk. Then I saw a bright green snake, long, slender fangs bared, slithering down the neck of the lamp toward me. "Holy shit!" I threw myself back in the chair, nearly tipping over.

Then I realized the snake wasn't actually moving. Looking more closely, I saw that its fangs were propped open with a stick. I heard someone snickering. I looked around, and there was Pancho's smiling face, poking around the side of the big map.

"You like that shaky snake, Lieutenant."

> Dear Mom and Dad,
> The other night I had to have dinner with all these awful Colonels—it was revolting.
> But we caught a beautiful green snake—a bamboo viper. It's terrifying

but dead. I shall bug you with another request. For some perverse reason I would like to have a book on snakes—Asian ones wit' pitchers. Things sound fair to middling at the Kidder mansion (but you have never seen such a beautiful bright green snake. A one-stepper—he bites you and you take one step, which sounds very scary, but they are pretty timid—it's the first snake I've seen over here—my Sgt. killed it with a machete).

R & R

———++———

THE INVESTIGATOR FROM NHA TRANG, A mild-mannered captain who looked too old to be a captain, spent three days with us, three days of hangovers for me at least—I took him every night to the Officers Club at the Chu Lai airfield. The day he left he told me he'd recommend "a slap on the wrist," and I felt relieved to hear that news again.

Our routines resumed. In the evening, there was **Combat!** and my map work and drinking in the lounge. Also a board game called Diplomacy, which my mother had sent at my request. Each of us played a nation fighting World War I, forming secret alliances and breaking them; quite often we ended up shouting at one another. And during the daylight hours, there were chores, such as the replacement of our rotting sandbags. The men hated filling new ones, maybe because it resembled work they'd had to do at stateside Army posts. They could work at filling sandbags for two hours and end up filling two apiece, unless I was shoveling alongside them. It had become a long-term project. I never thought to try to motivate them by pointing out that new sandbags might be vital to our survival. I only recall saying that new sandbags might be vital to our surviving inspections.

We hadn't suffered a lot of those, actually, but the threat of them seemed big to me, the threat of unknown consequences if an inspection went badly and also the threat to our privacy. I often mentioned the first, trying to reason with my men, and never named the second even to myself. It was only a feeling I had whenever some outsider, any outsider, visited our compound. The night, for instance, when the operations officer from our higher headquarters in Chu Lai came out, not to inspect us but for a social visit. He called me first. He told me he needed a break. He had never caused me any trouble. He'd even helped me. I should have been sympathetic. But I didn't feel hospitable when he arrived, and I'm sure it showed.

The men all wandered away, leaving us two officers alone in the lounge. I opened a couple of beers. We were chatting about college—he'd gone to Stanford—when Pancho sauntered in, carrying his blowtorch, which he proceeded to light. He brushed his black hair out of his eyes—it was getting too long again—and he began applying the flame to one of the interior plywood walls, scorching a patch, then lowering the torch and peering at the wood, examining the effect, all as if he hadn't even noticed us sitting there.

"**What** is that man doing?" the operations officer said to me in a loud whisper, over the hissing of the torch. He seemed alarmed. He must have thought, not unreasonably, that this man might be about to set the hootch on fire.

Later, Pancho would tell me, "If you heat up plywood, it makes it look dark, makes it look better." At the moment, though, I had no idea what he was up to. I looked at the operations officer, and I shrugged. There was smugness in that shrug. At the radio research compound in Chu Lai, officers didn't drink with enlisted men. But on a recent visit there, I had made a point of mingling with EM at their club. This distinguished me from my guest, the operations officer, I felt.

In fact, my visit to the EM club hadn't gone very well. One guy, not one of my own men, had said to me, in a friendly voice, "You were raised on a silver spoon, weren't you, Lieutenant?" I was in their club. I couldn't pull rank. All I could do was say, "Not really," while I remembered that, in fact, there was a little silver spoon at home that one of my grandparents had given to my mother when I was born. Actually, I'd felt relieved when the company commander had asked me not to intrude again on the enlisted club when I visited Chu Lai.

The operations officer and I stared at Pancho. The hissing had stopped. Pancho was staring at the blowtorch, muttering, "Flatdick thing isn't working right." Then he sauntered out the door.

I began to talk to the operations officer about my feeling for enlisted men.

After a while he said, "You're very malleable."

Forget it, I told myself after he left. Who cares what that asshole thinks?

THE WINTER MONSOON BEGAN IN OCTOBER. IF the scudding clouds tore open and a hazy sun appeared for a moment, one of us would shout and we'd all run outside, then hurry back in when it began to pour again. We wore our heavy field jackets indoors and walked to meals in olive-drab ponchos, slogging through mud, Spikes saying to me, "Y'all hear that great suckin' sound, Lieutenant?" He was saying the sound of our boots expressed his feelings toward the Army. It wasn't something an enlisted man, especially a sergeant, would say to every lieutenant. I'd smile as he said it, turning to his shrouded figure beside me.

Can the mud really have come halfway up my calves as I watched the men work on our malfunctioning generators? Looking back at meteorological records, I realize that the rainy season around Chu Lai that year was a great deal shorter than I have remembered, but it left a strong impression. **Ivory Fields** occurs in a hot, dry time, but in the prologue the narrator says, "When the ground that machines have eaten turns to mud and roads become swift streams and the rivers swell and the wind and rain drive helicopters right out of the sky, rain will own the land again. Then men will not move much except as other legged creatures move. It has always been that way and always will be in the few days left to come. So consider the rain. Without it the pride of foreign soldiers would be unbounded and the land might be left no pride at all."

There were in fact some days when the war from our vantage point came nearly to a halt, days when I had no fixes to report and, as Hemingway might have put it, I had too much time to think.

Letters from Mary Anne had dwindled. The ones that did arrive had grown increasingly cheerful and chatty, and they gave me an ominous feeling. She had suggested gently once—I didn't remember the occasion—that I should be a man, not a boy. For months I'd been trying to convince myself, by convincing everyone back home, that in the crucible of war I'd made that great transition. The actual facts of the case had a way of ganging up on me in the doorway of my hootch, when I walked down there alone after my morning briefing and breakfast at the H-Troop mess hall. The screen door would slam behind me, and I'd hear myself say aloud, "Shot in the head." I didn't know when I'd first uttered the phrase. I didn't wonder about that, but was always startled hearing it in my voice. I wasn't imagining suicide. I wasn't imagining myself dying in a glorious firefight. Originally, perhaps, I had imagined mourners at my funeral, but by now they were just magic words. "Shot in the head." Usually, this cleared the air for a while.

I spent hours alone in my hootch, the canvas flaps lowered, the rain ringing down on the metal roof, sometimes matching the rhythm I made on the manual typewriter. I finished a story about a soldier in an unnamed country who gets enraged when a fellow soldier tells him that human beings can't travel at the speed of light. His buddies don't know that he has just received in the mail a clipping of a wedding announcement from his hometown paper. He reads it again and he thinks: "She would be lying on her back, her legs spread, making little noises. And in his mind's eye his cute little girl, with her neat hair and little nose and pretty little round-collared blouse, tossing feverishly, naked below the waist."

Christmas was coming. I walked up to the Military Affiliate Radio Station, where a soldier could sometimes place an international call, a laborious process but free of charge. I had it in mind to call Mary Anne in the States. I tried, but no one answered.

"Sorry, Lieutenant," said the man who placed the call.

I walked back to our compound, feeling blue until the camera started following me again: reopening the letter I'd received back in October from David Riggs at Harvard.

> Strange the way Vietnam has all of a sudden ceased to be hard news. Every night at ten to seven Walter Cronkite switches over to some correspondent in khakis, standing in a sort of vacant lot, who proceeds to explain (usually with appropriate boom-boom sound effects) how Charlie has some new gear from Peking, or how we are building brand new villages out of corrugated aluminum . . . And for some reason (frustration, boredom? the Fall of that

pompous, good man Senator Eugene McCarthy?) everybody has decided that the war is just part of the system, like taxes, etc. Even radicals prefer to foment against abstractions—Our Warmongering Society—rather than to bother their heads about the miserable country in which you are stationed. I am afraid this means that you are being cheated—sent to a situation that, morally, is so desperate that no one wants any part of it. . . .

It might have felt good enough to imagine myself a young man risking his life for a noble cause, but to be a young man in a morally desperate situation that everyone back home wants to forget—this had a sweet sadness that reminded me of the most important of my literary experiences of war. Mainly Hemingway's **A Farewell to Arms** and his stories "In Another Country" and "A Way You'll Never Be," love and illusion destroyed by war. So much war fiction managed to deplore and romanticize at the same time.

It didn't really matter that I wasn't in much danger. Most of my correspondents back home didn't seem to know about the distinction between combat duty and duty like mine, between the lives of REMFs and those of grunts. To them, it seemed, any job in Vietnam must resemble the assault on Iwo

Jima. I'd reassured my correspondents in letters to the World, but then, often enough, I'd left room for doubt: "I have a sore ear and some boils, but otherwise I am very healthy. Go's brother died of something I can't mention in a letter, and I just told him. But I have all my shots, don't worry."

I wrote to Mary Anne. Soon I would be eligible for a week of rest and recuperation, R & R. I thought she might meet me in Hawaii. I wrote the letter carefully. In the first draft I wrote, "Perhaps I already asked once—I think I did. No harm done. I will understand if you choose not to, and am quite through with turning pleasant ideas into nasty ones. I feel myself a very jolly person now—my company is highly coveted, by man and beast, general and private, easterner and westerner. Well, to enjoy yourself you have to be a little bit of a fool." She wrote back saying she couldn't come. I sensed that she was sad, and I knew she wasn't telling me all she felt. She closed with her signature, without writing the word **Love.**

I knew that she loved me, but in a way that had grown more sisterly than romantic. The fact was unacceptable. It made me furious. A few days later, I woke up with a fever. I sent a message back to the company saying I was sick. I drank like Tex that night, and staggered down to my hootch afterward and wrote this:

Dear Mary Anne,

Many days have passed, and several nights which I cannot recall with any certainty. One time I stood on the top of the hill when mortar rounds were falling with their little muffled thumps throughout the base camp. Other people were dying who did not want to. I wanted to see. Now I do not want to die, but I like to live this way, I really do, and I think I am best suited for the kind of certainty of war. You know who are enemies and you do not have friends. You expect nothing from people and give nothing, but you watch and see and soon you know all about stern dictums, such as, "Be a man, not a boy." Still I believe in things—loyalty, honesty, honor, courage—but having never seen them, except once in myself, I prefer their opposites. I prefer them, that is, to the in-betweens, the rationalizers—"it's better this way"—and their lack of all courage. Because it takes some courage to be disloyal and deny it to yourself. The good person owes people something—hatred, love, honesty—what he would extend, or like extended, to himself, or herself.

I do not care for you or about you any longer, nor will I ever again. But I would like you to know that I do thoroughly hate you, and that, at least, is something. You have a maudlin, deceitful mind, and you are cruel no matter how kind to children. In the end those things do not distinguish you.

This is your receipt. What you may have done to me, or I to you, in the past, is nothing alongside this little agony you built by neglect. And you will not understand why, or what that means. It's gone now, and as a matter of fact it came and went swiftly. But I believed in you, and in being good and fine, in punishments and rewards, not as absolutes but fine contingencies, and I could have spent my life on them if you had paid me only the respect which I have richly deserved from you, and you had taken leave of me honorably.

Do not come near me and do not write me a reply, or I will make you and whatever you love this month very sorry; and I mean that as you only can when you know your capabilities.

I have nothing to lose. I really lost my virginity over here. I shot a man through the head and little pieces of his brain and a great quantity of blood colored my gun and my clothes and my face. I never cried so hard over you. But, not unlike you, I am becoming a whore of a different sort. I like it. I LIKE it. You filthy, rotten bitch. One letter from you at any one time would have done so much for me. You fucking bitch.

Then I lay on my cot with my .45 locked and loaded and resting on my chest. I yelled now and then. I heard the rats. The next morning, I made it to the colonel's briefing, then fell back into my cot in my hootch. My men let me sleep. But by noon the air inside was like an oven. I woke up bathed in sweat. I read over the letter. It seemed better not to mail it. I just had a short-term virus, as it turned out. But I didn't always take the malaria pills. So, I told myself, it could have been something much worse.

The rains ended. Life returned to normal, hot afternoons, dust that stiffened your hair. One of the commo ops played a Simon and Garfunkel tape again and again, inside the operations hootch, while manning the Teletype. I still wasn't tired of the songs. "Scarborough Fair." "Homeward Bound." "Feelin' Groovy." Elsewhere, life was full of possibility. I fell for the songs every time, wistful for things I imagined people my age were doing back home.

Back when I'd gone to the ville with my men, I had waited outside while they visited the prostitutes. Two would approach the truck. "Boomboom, GI? You want fucky-fucky?" Recently, a command decision had made it illegal to perform "Hollywood stops" (not fully stopping at intersections; the generals were upset about the frequency of accidents), and getting caught with a prostitute was now an arrestable offense. I certainly didn't want to get arrested myself, but I didn't forbid my men to go to the ville. One of them had already contracted gonorrhea twice from the same woman. Many others got crab lice. Spikes would tell them, "Here's what you do, bud. Shave your crotch on one side, pour lighter fluid on the hairy side, set it on fire, and when they come out of the brush, stab 'em with an ice pick." One morning I found a crab in my groin, without having done anything to deserve it. GIs from other outfits were using my private shitter, which was situated rather near the main base camp road. I found several of them, tough-looking grunts, standing outside it in a line one day and very politely asked them not to use it anymore. "It's okay this time," I said.

For me, R & R seemed to promise the best and safest opportunity for meeting compliant young women. At the detachment, new guys listened to old guys tell stories about their trips. Tex, for instance, used to talk about his R & R in Taipei. "The Peito Baths are beaucoup number one. All you do is ask a taxi driver." He would describe a delicate Asian woman giving him a massage, during one part of which she walked on his back, up and down his spine. "Yeah, Tex, and what else?" He wouldn't reveal more. "Didn't get any, huh, Tex?" He would smile. He'd get a faraway look. "Go to Taipei, the Peito Baths, bud. All you do is ask the taxi driver."

But hearing Tex talk about those baths in Taipei, I kept getting a picture of a large, unsanitary public steam bath, with tiled walls like those in decaying New York City subway stations. We could choose from among any number of places. Sydney, Australia, for instance. Someone had heard someone else say that Sydney was **the** place to go. "Round-eyes meet you at the plane. No shit. They practically fuck you right there." But I thought I knew enough about round-eyed women to be skeptical of that. I had been reading more of Joseph Conrad. "Singapore." The name on our list made me think of sampans, courageous sea captains, women in sarongs. One of my men was also eligible for R & R at this time. That was Schulzie. We decided to go to Singapore together.

No trace of Schulzie appears in **Ivory Fields**. Perhaps because he became a real friend to me, he became in retrospect less colorful than others. He was a lean, angular guy who often spoke a street-wise lingo from the side of his mouth that I assumed he'd come by honestly, growing up around New York. "Didn't your mother ever teach you nothin'?" "Money talks, Jack." "That don't mean jackshit." "Fool me once, mothah, shame on you . . ." But it wasn't entirely convincing. I have a photo of him and me that describes him better. We stand bare-chested by our truck. My right hand is raised. I had sent a copy of the picture to Mary Anne, in part because I thought I looked hand-some in it, and in part to prove I wasn't paranoid, that I was having a real good time in spite of every-thing. I wrote on the back: "Speaking Cherokee with Schulzie. I have been informed of my nomi-nation as a third rate Cherokee deity, by Schulzie, who was informed via letter by his blood brother, Catcher Bear. It is a great honor and a heavy responsibility." I never felt worried about my standing with Schulzie. I found genuine relief in his silliness. He was still open to the world.

On the short plane ride to Da Nang, I told him to call me by my first name, for the time being, during R & R. In Da Nang, we parted for the night, Schulzie to the enlisted barracks, I to the officers' quarters, Schulzie saying, "By this time tomorrow night, you and me are gonna be gettin' laid!"

"And drunk!"

We nudged each other and went our separate ways.

A briefing officer had warned us that more than one soldier had gone to sleep here on his way to R & R and awakened to find his wallet gone, the buttoned pocket where he'd stashed it neatly scissored away. So the place felt weird even before I went to the officers' latrine and read, on the inside of the door, an argument in graffiti that went like this: "The First Air Cav. saved the Marines' ass again in Khe Sanh." This insult was signed by a U.S. Army captain. Right below it came the retort, signed by a Marine Corps major: "The United States Army has never, repeat never, saved the Marines! Semper Fi, asshole!"

The barracks were dimly lit. Rows of single beds covered with olive- drab scratchy wool blankets and crisp sheets. A place where strangers slept side by side. A place full of rumors of war, war at various levels. A few years later, I wrote up notes of my memories of the night I spent in that place. In them, I describe sleeping in a roomful of officers, my bunk next to the bunk of a young infantry lieutenant, who lay with the sheet pulled up to his chin and talked softly to the ceiling, saying aloud, "But it wasn't exactly a bad smell. You could tell they were graves when we found them, and when we reported it, the S-2 said to dig them up. The S-2 wanted to know what killed them. They want to know if it was artillery or air strikes that killed them whenever you find graves, so they can say who gets the kills. Wounds have a funny smell, too. I can always tell if someone's wounded just by sniffing." Reading this, conversing with my memories, I feel as though I'm looking down a long corridor and sense something in the shadows at the end.

The next morning a sergeant led a large group of us onto the tarmac of the huge Da Nang air-field. He yelled instructions. I heard him say that enlisted men and officers would ride in different parts of the plane. I must have stopped listening, because I was in my seat—a commercial airliner seat—when the sergeant said, "Is there someone on this plane who **isn't** going to Hawaii?"

I walked fast down the aisle, feeling eyes on me, keeping mine straight ahead. The sergeant seemed more mystified than angry. "Sir, didn't you hear me say this plane was for Hawaii?"

Schulzie came up to me when I returned to the group for Singapore. He was grinning. I could tell he was trying not to crack up. "What were you doin', Lieutenant?"

I glared at him.

In a room at the Singapore airport, an Army major briefed us. "All right, listen up." They wanted us to have a good time. This was our chance to let off some steam. But Singapore was a big city, and they didn't want us getting in trouble. We could have our R & R canceled for driving a car, for . . . I didn't listen to the rest. Then he told us about the recommended hotels. "Stick with these hotels. You don't have to stay in them, but if you don't want to catch something . . ."

In that barren room at the airport, I had a feeling, which I didn't fully trust, that we were suddenly transformed into a crowd of equal rank, finally being offered something we all wanted, even the smattering of older guys, sergeants and officers in their thirties or early forties, all exploding in one great pent-up roar of laughter. I was more aware of hearing the laughter and of Schulzie's agitation beside me than of laughing myself. And yet I couldn't wait to get to one of those hotels.

The major said, "Every girl in the hotels on this list gets checked once a week."

"Who gets to check 'em?" somebody yelled from the crowd.

The major smiled. He said, when we quieted down, that we should remember we represented our country and our branches of service. "Now go have some fun!"

We had to choose our hotel right away. I was used to making decisions by now. Schulzie looked over my shoulder at the list. "What do you think, Trace?" One name stuck out. "Serene House."

On the bus, a handsome, dark-haired soldier sat beside us, scowling. Suddenly, he was talking to me and Schulzie. I guess he had to tell his story to someone. A week before, when his week of R & R was over, he tore up his identification card because someone had told him, correctly, that the government of Singapore wouldn't let him leave without one.

Schulzie couldn't believe it. That was too much good fortune.

"You think I'm shittin' you?" the young soldier said.

Every day he had to ride down to the airport in case his new card had arrived. Then he could go back to Serene House, where the military was paying his room and board. They couldn't prove he'd destroyed his ID card, so they couldn't punish him, he said. But it seemed as if they might as well have, because he'd run out of spending money. He'd met a girl at Serene House named Lea. He'd kept her for a week. He didn't have money to keep her now. But what he had with her wasn't like what other GIs had. What a girl. What a woman. No one better call her a whore. He'd tear up his new card when it came if he hadn't run out of money, he said. He might tear it up anyway, just to stay near her. He didn't ask us for a loan, and we didn't offer one. He gazed out the bus window in silence the rest of the way.

Serene House was a motel, three stories, I think, nothing exotic about it, except that a line of young Asian women stood in the lobby, all in high heels and miniskirts, elaborately made up. I heard someone say there were fifty, for only forty GIs. We rushed up to our rooms. "See ya later," said Schulzie. I didn't shower. I wanted to get back to the lobby before the others had taken the best-looking ones.

I saw the broke, dark-haired soldier standing in the lobby some distance away, beside a potted palm, staring at one of the girls in the lineup—his Lea, no doubt—and she seemed aware of his gaze and was making a point of not looking at him. She looked older and far less beautiful than some of the others. For example, the one I approached, a petite, black-haired girl in a miniskirt. I tried talking to her. She shied away. There was a sudden commotion, the girl turning and speaking to an older woman behind her, the madam, I guessed. I had no idea what the girl was saying—the language must have been Malay or Chinese—but she spoke rapidly and her voice sounded urgent.

The madam approached, speaking soothingly to her. The girl twisted away. Suddenly, she broke into English, no doubt for my benefit. "He isn't good-looking!"

The older woman answered sharply, succinctly,

fiercely, in Malay or Chinese. Then the girl stood motionless, head bowed.

It shakes one's confidence to be rejected by a prostitute. I look at that photograph of myself, standing bare-chested with Schulzie beside our truck at my detachment. I'm muscular, but not heavily. I don't seem to be carrying any fat at all. I'm a little over six feet. I have a full head of brown hair, a good chin, and no outlandish features, though if it weren't for the thatch of hair on my chest, I could have passed for sixteen. Standing there in the lobby of Serene House, I thought, It must be my glasses. I had worn them ever since I confessed to my first-grade teacher that I couldn't see the blackboard. I thought I was much better-looking without them on, when I looked in the mirror without them on. And I'd have taken them off before presenting myself to the prostitutes in Serene House, but I knew from unfortunate experiences at college dances that, when I had them off, all women were also much better-looking.

"Listen," I said to the madam, feeling heat in my cheeks. "No problem. Forget it."

"No, it's okay," said the madam. They all spoke good English, it seemed. "She's going with you."

What followed, almost at once, up in my room, might have occurred in a doctor's office, if there were ones set up for the purpose. A completely passive, naked girl on the bed, with a wiry bush that scratched a bit; brief exertions—there was something rubbery-feeling about her vagina—and afterward the return of dull sanity. I noticed, for instance, a box in the wall of my room through which Muzak, real department store Muzak, was piped. And cruel feelings toward the girl, who now seemed to take a livelier interest in me. I wanted to send her away, but I'd bought her for the night, and after I'd taken a shower and found her still there in the room, I thought I should get my money's worth, later on.

She, however, wanted to talk. About her family. She said she'd been forced into this business because her father had died, and she had to raise money to take care of her sick aunt. I don't remember with certainty, but I think I was planning to give her more money, until I started getting dressed to take her out to dinner and she threw another tantrum—this time about my sport jacket, blue with white buttons. She said it wasn't "good-looking." She was clearly quite young, in life and in her trade, a petulant teenager, remarkably straightforward.

I didn't rehire her. I saw Lea at a table in the barroom the next morning. I sat down and talked to her. Up at the bar several girls were working on my fellow soldiers, rubbing themselves against them, wriggling down onto their laps. Lea didn't do any of that. She seemed very grown-up, dignified actually, so that, after we'd talked for a time, I had to drop my eyes in order to ask if she was available.

Maybe I only imagined that when I walked out to the lobby with her, on the way to my room, I caught a glimpse of the dark-haired soldier. I didn't much care, to tell the truth. I have a clear memory, though, of seeing him from the lobby, maybe later that day or the next morning. The bus that had taken us from the airport was just leaving, and I saw his face in profile in one of the bus windows. He looked straight ahead. He looked scared to me, or as if he were trying not to look scared, as if he were being taken to jail.

Lea sat down on the edge of the bed. She patted a hand on the spread beside her. I sat down. She leaned forward and looked carefully at me. "I don't understand why that girl said you weren't good-looking." Then she undressed me.

She plumped up the pillows and gently pushed my head back on them, and I don't think it was possible to feel stiffer than I did, or more surprised—that she would do this, without even being asked—when her lips started gliding up and down the ventral side of my cock. This ridiculous thing, always embarrassing me as a schoolboy, now jutting up in the air, and here was this person treating it so respectfully, so tenderly. A hand reached up and covered my mouth.

I knew it was only right to reciprocate. This was a time long before AIDS. I didn't for a moment think about all the soldiers who had preceded me and, if the randiest of my men were at all representative, how many dangerous, unsavory places their cocks must have entered. I just knew that the noises she made were genuine, and that when, in due course, her small body shuddered, she was having an orgasm. My own was a triumph, a thunderous event, nothing that almost any young man celibate for six months couldn't have accomplished, but in that moment the universe made up for every wrong it had done me. Then I didn't want her anywhere near me, for a while.

Schulzie and I went on a double date that night, in Lea's car. She straightened my necktie before we left the room. She had me drive. Mary Anne had wanted me to change. Well, I had. No question about it. Driving a car, in spite of emphatic warnings from the authorities. In fact, this was pretty adventurous. Singapore had retained that vestige of contrary Englishness, left-hand-side driving. It was tricky.

Lea had chosen a fancy restaurant. It was clear at the door that the women with us weren't entirely welcome. I seem to remember an explanation from Lea that had to do with the fact that she and Schulzie's escort were Malaysian, not Chinese. I suppose there was a more obvious problem. Anyway, I sensed that Lea enjoyed the slight discomfort we caused, lifting her chin to the head-waiter, smiling slightly when he turned and led us to a table.

Schulzie's choice of girl surprised me. She was scrawny. I kept thinking, She looks like a chicken. I thought he'd probably hire a different girl the next day. But he rode to the restaurant with his arm around her in the backseat, and escorted her in on the crook of his arm. I felt embarrassed for him, until I'd had a few drinks. I did the driving back to Serene House. At one point, Lea cried out in panic and grabbed the wheel, and we swerved away from oncoming headlights just in time. I don't think Schulzie noticed. He was necking in the backseat.

The next morning I woke up to find Lea get-ting out of the bath. I said I was hoping she would stay in bed awhile. She said she was sorry, but she had to go. She didn't say why. She didn't say she had to take care of an ailing relative. She would come back that evening. Did I want her for another night? I said I wasn't sure. She said she had to know.

I grew up in an era when, at least in that vast, amorphous social region carved out by returning World War II soldiers, or at least in my town, or maybe just in my own interior world, what was called "getting bare tit off a girl" ranked as an achievement you wanted to tell everyone all about, but only on the night when it happened. Waking up the next morning, a boy of my era was apt to think, Uh-oh. A line had been crossed, a commitment made. A boy had only two options: accept it and carry the girl's books to class or, my early solution, stay as far away from her as possible. I told Lea I just wasn't sure. When she left, I felt elated. By the time I went downstairs to find Schulzie, I wondered if I'd made a mistake.

We sat at the bar, Schulzie and I and another young soldier.

"These girls. Does every one of them have a sick aunt or uncle or something?"

Schulzie put his head back and howled.

"They try that on you, too?" the other soldier asked.

"Fuckin' A!" Schulzie banged his fist on the bar. This was the Schulzie who talked from the side of his mouth. "That's all they want. The green stuff. Fuckin' whores." And he said it so knowingly and with such a leer that the true import of this, the innocence of it, went right past, and we all laughed.

"How come it's never her father or mother, or one of her kids?"

"That's true. I don't know. I wonder why."

"Maybe there's something about their religion. You can't tell a lie about a really close relative."

What was their religion? I ought to see Singapore. Schulzie said he didn't feel like it. His girl was coming back in an hour or so. I went for a long walk alone. I saw one temple, gaudily painted, and got a glimpse of some fishing boats from a bridge. I started out with the stranger's edginess and after a while realized I was utterly safe in that modern-looking city, where, as Lea had told me, you could be arrested for spitting in public. I was careful not to throw my cigarette butts in the gutter. I followed a pretty Western-looking woman, a round-eye, for a few blocks, imagining that I might pick her up. I stopped at a tailor's and got myself measured for a white linen suit. Back on the streets, I saw a sign for something called the American Club. Inside, a middle-aged Brit—he was in oil, he said—bought me a drink, and his wife set me straight about the general shiftiness of Malaysians.

I got back to Serene House in time for "The Suzy Wong Show," a small Asian woman up on the stage, doing a complete striptease. Total nakedness in public was still risqué, indeed illegal in most of America. There were hoots and hollers and many shining faces of drunk GIs, but more who now looked like men with their wives, standing with the whores they'd hired at the back of the room, laughing and clapping, but rather sedately, as if at a floor show in Las Vegas. I saw Lea. She walked past on the arm of a tall black man with a mustache, a sergeant, probably. I was impressed, in one way. Several girls I had talked to said they didn't like to go with black soldiers, with "spades," as they called them. She didn't seem uncomfortable. She didn't seem to make a point of not noticing me. I thought she might not remember me.

The madam pursued me. Maybe I didn't like girls, she said. I ended up with a wiry one, who went about her business cheerfully but quickly and tidily, as if it were housekeeping. I had drunk a fair amount, and I felt like doing something I would have done back home. I felt like reading aloud to her. I had brought along my collected Yeats. I read "The Second Coming." "Isn't that great?"

She looked puzzled.

"Sorry," I said.

No, no, she said. She liked it. It's possible, of course, that she did, that the music of Yeats reached her more deeply than it did me. No doubt she preferred a poetry reading to further mandatory sex. I didn't care. I lay in my bed in Serene House, a young woman against my shoulder, her hair so stiff from spray it felt like a rash on my skin, and I read some of Yeats's poems about art, until she fell asleep.

I hadn't talked to more than a few other soldiers. But Schulzie had been making new friends.

The next day he took me to meet a couple of them, who were sharing a room in Serene House. Two grinning young GIs, naked save for underpants, sat side by side at the head of a king-size bed. One held a bottle of whiskey by the neck. Three young Asian women, in bras and panties, lay as if scattered around the room, one on the floor, laughing, clearly drunk, another in an armchair, with a woozy smile on her face, another curled up on the foot of the bed and fast asleep.

A year later, when I wrote **Ivory Fields,** I was newly sensitive to the plight of oppressed Asian women. After all, Lieutenant Dempsey's story turns on his attempt to stop the rape of a Vietnamese girl. But I can't claim to have had such feelings at Serene House. Schulzie and I walked out, and he started laughing about the scene behind us. Those two GIs, he said, had holed up with those three girls, and for the past four days they'd hardly left their room.

"We should've done that," Schulzie said.

"Yeah, we should have."

But Schulzie was still employing the same girl. I sat beside him in the bar and listened as he and another young soldier complained about the time these women spent curling their hair. We went out together in a taxi. Schulzie's girl came along. I thought she was going to show us the town, but it turned out to be a shopping trip, Schulzie sitting in the backseat with his arm around her, making sour faces whenever she ordered the driver to make another stop. Schulzie shaking his head, saying to me, "Women, you know?" He wasn't alone in any of this. Maybe the name of our hotel had something to do with it. All around Serene House I saw soldiers walking hand in hand with their prostitutes, pecking them on the cheeks, retiring after the local floor show around 10:00 P.M., playing out what seemed like parodies of American conjugal life. And I discovered, if you went out into the hallways after ten or so, you'd usually run into a girl who had found a way to take a break from her employer. Black-haired young women in miniskirts, interchangeable to me by this time. "You want a short-timer?" they'd ask.

"How much?"

I contented myself with short-timers for the rest of our vacation. It's hard to break out of the kind of bitter mood that keeps looking for reasons to justify its existence. In time you may really believe that the worst you can imagine about everything human must be true, simply because it is the worst. At any rate, I'd found a way to make sure I wouldn't be disappointed. Schulzie seemed cheerful on the trip back from Singapore. I actually felt glad to return to our compound, metal roofs dotted with rotting sandbags, Simon and Garfunkel playing on the commo op's tape deck, a basin of cold water right around dawn on the stoop of the operations hootch, the confusion I felt when I saw my face in my pocket-size mirror. Voices called out, "One hundred ninety-nine days to DEROS." "Seventy-three and counting. Eat your heart out, new guys." The ultimate in destinations was, in Spikes's phrase, "the land of the big PX and the all-night generator." Pancho called it "Fort Home." There was still a place where life was perfect.

OPERATIONS

———❚———

I WAS WORKING ON ANOTHER SHORT STORY—
about a soft-spoken soldier, not exactly like
me, I thought, but like the person I was coming to resemble, who, in an indefinite place a lot
like Vietnam, befriends a semiretarded Army cook
and meets a tragic end through kindness. I had
worked on it all morning in my hootch. When I
came up to operations, I found a couple of new
fixes for North Vietnamese units, close to each
other and not very far from one of our battalion
base camps to the west. The fixes were several
hours old.

When I pulled up in the jeep outside the TOC,

that big igloo of sandbags, Colonel Mahoney was on his way out the door, walking rather slowly for him. I showed him the new locations. He stared at the map. Then he looked up at me, and I thought that I saw sadness in his face. "I wish I'd had these earlier," he said. There had been a firefight an hour or so ago, right near those locations, he explained. If he'd known the enemy units were there in force, he'd have sent in air strikes and reinforcements. He said he'd lost a couple of men. There was no rancor in his voice. He wondered why the locations had come to us so late.

"I don't know, sir. But I'll find out," I said.

I went back and spent half an hour in the lounge, drinking beer and telling Spikes what had happened, saying I should have brought those fixes to the colonel sooner. I wondered if I was to blame for the deaths of those GIs. I went to operations and wondered to the commo op, a boy named Rose. He looked at the messages that contained the fixes. "Hey, Lieutenant, look when these came in." It was true that they'd arrived at my detachment about half an hour before I'd taken them to Colonel Mahoney, but Rose pointed out to me, those new locations had languished in Chu Lai for about three hours before the commo ops back there had sent them out to us. Rose was a chatty young man, too eager to please. As it happened, he had spent time as a commo op in Chu Lai, and I think the other commo ops back there had picked on him. At the moment, though, it didn't occur to me that he might be harboring a grudge.

There was often a moment, a beer or two short of drunkenness, when I could hear my voice grow loud and brassy, and I liked the sound. Then, in my mind, partial beliefs tended to become whole. Generally, these resembled the beliefs of whoever was around. I drank another beer. Then I drafted a message to the operations officer, denouncing the commo ops in Chu Lai. Because of them, American soldiers had died today, I wrote.

I showed it to Rose. "Think I should send this?"

"Yeah!"

Only minutes later, the operations officer called me on the landline phone. I had no right to send a message like that, he said. Then my company commander called. "I can't believe a person with your education would send that message. I think if you were here right now in Chu Lai, some of these men would shoot you." This was very strong language, a taboo broken, for a commander to talk about fragging that way.

I apologized to the captain, and to the commo ops in Chu Lai in another message. "Shot in the head," I said in the doorway of my hootch when I turned in that night, but the words didn't help much. Why did I have to overreact? Why couldn't I just do my job and not worry about what other people did? Why did I have to dabble in causes I didn't really care about?

Strangely enough, my outburst improved our operation. The commo ops in Chu Lai weren't lazy, and weren't to blame for the delay. There was simply too much traffic passing through their Teletypes. Within days, the operations officer initiated new procedures for getting fixes to me, so that most would come not through the Chu Lai comm center but by secure radio from the direction-finding plane itself. Now locations would get to the colonel sooner. Enemy soldiers, presumably, would have less time to get away.

I HAD TURNED TWENTY-THREE IN NOVEMBER AND now wore on my collar the first lieutenant's black bar—black in a combat zone, silver elsewhere. Promotion to first lieutenant came automatically after a year of active duty, unless you did something very wrong, lost a secret code word message, for instance. But my promotion had come through right on time. Soon afterward I'd been ordered to report to Colonel Riddle in Nha Trang.

He handed me a couple of official letters from across his desk. One was signed by Colonel

Mahoney: "As I leave this command I would like to extend this letter of commendation for a most outstanding performance of duty." It went on in that vein for a few paragraphs and closed, "A copy of this letter will be placed in both your branch and permanent 201 files." This, I understood, would help if I decided to make the Army my career.

The other letter was signed by Colonel Riddle. It read in part, "Your dedication and enthusiasm in providing the best possible special intelligence support to the 198th Light Infantry Brigade reflect most creditably upon your unit, the Radio Research community as a whole, and most importantly, upon yourself. I am sure I can count on you for continued high standards of performance, and shall be looking to you as an example of other personnel of this command."

"Thank you, sir."

Then he handed me the letter of reprimand. I felt his eyes on me and composed a sorrowful expression, playing my part and believing in it for a moment, as I read of my "gross carelessness" and "the violation of trust" I had committed, endangering the lives of American soldiers by allowing the loss of a classified message. I looked up, my eyes, I remember clearly, actually stinging, and saw that he was smiling. Was it the smile itself that was sickening or the reassurance that it offered? I was quite recovered. He reached for the paper, I handed it to him, he held it aloft in front of me and, still smiling, tore it in half.

"Thank you, sir."

He dismissed me, saying, "Don't let me down now, boy."

Just making sure I realized I was in his debt. "No, sir."

I had lingered in the briefing room on Colonel Mahoney's last morning, standing nearby as he thanked his senior staff. He praised each for his "loyalty," using the word in the personal sense. I didn't know anything but rumors about the lives of full-bull colonels, but I imagined the years it took to arrive at the rank, years of holding your tongue and smiling at people you despised, years that could be ruined by one or two commanders who disliked you or by a wife who drank too much. There would be years of preparation— weeklong maneuvers and mock battles; classes on the doctrines of Metternich, the tactics of Patton, at the Army War College. You'd dream of the day when you would command your own brigade in an actual war. But your chance in Vietnam was brief, because so many other full-bull colonels were waiting for their turns.

No wonder Colonel Mahoney got a little over-wrought now and then. He wasn't the sort of man who invited pity, but I remembered feeling sorry for him once. He had been briefing the Americal Division's commanding general here in this room, and he'd gotten carried away and tapped the general on the knee with his branding iron, and I'd noticed the general stiffen slightly and shift his burly torso.

"Sir," I had said, stepping forward. "I just want to say goodbye."

"Oh, yes. Lieutenant Kidder. You did well, too."

"Thank you, sir." Perhaps he had sensed my sincerity, though at the time I didn't think he could possibly remember the reason for it.

I was grateful to the small, natty colonel, but he'd never been a rival to my other older friends, Sam and David. He had too many traits I thought I recognized in myself. Besides, I disapproved of colonels.

The new brigade commander was named Colonel Chamberlain. I sized him up from the back of the briefing room. He was tall, which might be an improvement. He also seemed comparatively relaxed in the commander's chair. And instead of a swagger stick, he had a stutter. Colonel Mahoney used to get my attention, but by the time this new colonel finished stammering and framed a sentence, he also had my sympathy. It would be hard to get through basic training with a speech impediment, I thought, remembering six-foot-six-inch Sergeant Fisher and the other drill sergeants I had known. When my turn came to brief him and I introduced myself, the new colonel gave me a small, friendly smile, tinged with amusement, perhaps.

"I think we're going to like this colonel," I told Spikes back at the detachment. "We should invite him over for cocktails some afternoon." Spikes liked the idea. He and I cleaned up the lounge, and the colonel actually accepted. He didn't stay long, but he stood at our homemade bar in that hootch and had a glass of bourbon and water with me. At one point I said to him, "I know a lot of officers don't trust enlisted men, but these guys are great."

He lowered his head and looked at me from the upper quadrant of his eyes, as if looking over the rims of glasses, in the way Robert Fitzgerald had looked at me when I'd aroused his skepticism. "Yea-yea-yea-yes, but your men aren't like most infantrymen."

I had considered discussing my moral objections to the Vietnam War with him until he said that.

Some nights later it happened again, the commo op on duty calling through my screen walls after midnight that a new fix had come in. The new system with the direction-finding plane was not infallible. Some fixes still arrived many hours late. This time I went alone to the colonel's house trailer. One of the first things Colonel Chamberlain had done was to get his quarters out of the bunkered pit in the ground. Maybe he just didn't like the feeling of sleeping half underground. But I thought he wanted to make himself as vulnerable to incoming as the other soldiers on LZ Bayonet. He was sitting on his bed in the house trailer, just as Colonel Mahoney had some months before. The new colonel rubbed the crew-cut top of his head with the knuckles of one hand, rubbed vigorously. Then he smiled. "Guh-guh-good morning, Lieutenant."

"Good morning, sir. Sir, this just came in." I handed him the map. On it was a dot perilously close to our base camp. It was that troublesome 3d NVA Regiment again.

He studied the map for a time. Then he looked at me again. "Well, Lieutenant, wha-wha-what would **you** do?"

A colonel of infantry asking a young intelligence officer what he would do? It was unheard of. For a moment I was tempted to make something up, and then I knew I shouldn't. It's always possible to borrow from the character of someone you've decided to admire.

He was still looking at me, eyebrows slightly lifted.

"I don't know, sir." I wet my lips. "I'm not a tactician."

A smile crinkled up the weathered skin around his eyes. "Nuh-nuh-**neither** am I!"

That location was just another false alarm. On the big map in the operations hootch, the war seemed to have reached stasis. I still wrote letters home in which I said that the North Vietnamese might be planning new offensives, but I saw no evidence of that. On occasion I heard of incidents that might have qualified as battles, or massacres. The night, for instance, when an NVA battalion tried to assault Tam Ky City and were slaughtered while attempting to cross the coastal plain by that "they-kill-VC" armored cavalry regiment. (Several hundred corpses dotted the ground, I heard from an MI lieutenant who had flown over the battlefield. I remember corpses being dumped at the helicopter pad in the base camp like sacks of grain from a chopper, to be searched and identified, I assumed.) But most of what I heard about were skirmishes, and most of those, it seemed, went badly for our side.

One time I went into the TOC to bring the S-3 another of those "on the move" documents—triple-wrapped so it couldn't blow away—and found Colonel Chamberlain inside talking on the radio. To a company commander, I gathered, who was caught in an ambush somewhere out in those hills to the west.

"Mu-mu-move!" the colonel was saying into the microphone in his hand.

The radio crackled. The infantry captain's voice

came into the room, along with sounds that took me back to basic training and the live-fire exercise when we had to crawl under barbed wire while a machine gun, fixed in place, fired real bullets over our heads, a sound nowhere near as loud as something designed to kill you ought to make. The embattled captain's voice had a timbre I admired, one I didn't think I could reproduce in his position. He didn't sound entirely calm, but he wasn't screaming. He said, over the crackling radio, "It's like pulling teeth, trying to move."

Colonel Chamberlain keyed his mike. "Stu-stop pulling teeth, and move!"

I began to feel as if I were a bystander at a traffic accident, all too fascinated. I left soon afterward, before hearing how the fight ended. I heard fragmentary accounts of other horrors like that one at almost every morning's briefing, reports of American platoons and rifle companies walking into ambushes, and of American soldiers losing limbs to booby traps, often on the Batangan Peninsula, just north of the towns of My Lai, an area known collectively as Pinkville both because it was depicted in pink on the map and because it was what was known as a "VC stronghold." The massacre of civilians at My Lai had already occurred, but the bodies were still buried and its public revelation was still the better part of a year away. To me, Pinkville wasn't yet a place where

Vietnamese women were raped and babies shot. It was just another battleground where American combat soldiers got maimed. A notorious place around brigade headquarters.

On our map in the operations hootch, the Batangan Peninsula was a little cape jutting into the South China Sea. A yellow dot with a red center, like a cartoon eye—Rosenthal, I think, had invented all such symbols—moved around it. Sometimes a brown dot with a red center lingered near the yellow one. The brown dot depicted the 38th Main Force Vietcong Battalion, but it usually drifted south of our AO, and it wasn't often on the air. The yellow one with the red center stood for the 48th Main Force Vietcong Battalion, and it was much more active, presumably more important. We got fixes on its radio maybe two days out of seven. Once in a great while it traveled a few kilometers south of Pinkville, but mainly it stayed on the peninsula, tracing patterns on my map which suggested that it ruled the place. I thought perhaps the NVA colonels had their own words of praise for it; maybe at their briefings they would say, "That Forty-eighth Battalion, they kill Americans."

EARLY IN THE NEW YEAR, UNFAMILIAR FACES appeared at the morning briefing, faces rising out of tailored fatigues. They brought my colonel news of a large new operation, planned in Da Nang at the office of the commanding general of the 3d Marine Amphibious Force. I found a document containing the contents of that briefing many years later, in the archives of the U.S. Army War College in Pennsylvania, a once-secret document that the archivist declassified on the spot—another piece of paper that had floated away, now in an old metal filing cabinet in the basement of an Army building. It came in capital letters and numbered paragraphs. The document began, as follows:

1. (S) THE ACCELERATED PACIFICATION CAMPAIGN IS MOVING AHEAD WELL. . . .
2. (S) THE TOP PRIORITY TARGET AREA IN THE BATANGAN REGION REFERRED TO AS PINK VILLE IS STILL COMPLETELY UNDER VC/NVA CONTROL. . . . THE TOTAL ESTIMATED POPULATION THERE IS 27,470. ESTIMATED ENEMY FORCES INCLUDE TWO VC/NVA BATTALIONS, TWO TO FOUR VC/NVA COMPANIES AND A HUNDRED OR MORE LOCAL GUERRILLAS. WE HOLD BLACKLISTS CONTAINING NAMES OF 208 VCI. VC/NVA FORCES IN REGION HAVE CAPABILITY TO MOUNT BATTALION SIZE COORDINATED ATTACKS ANYWHERE IN THE TARGET REGION. SMALL UNIT

HARASSING ATTACKS ARE OCCURRING
ON A WEEKLY BASIS. . . .

The plan was to deal with those battalions and
companies and Vietcong Irregulars once and for
all. A huge force would be assembled, U.S. Marines and infantry from the Americal Division,
and also South Vietnamese troops, nearly eleven
thousand men in all. They would cordon off the
entire enemy stronghold. They'd make an armed
wall of troops eleven miles long, over hills and
flooded rice paddies, all the way across the throat
of the peninsula. Navy Swift Boats would patrol
the coast.

Once the cordon was in place, helicopters
would circle over the impounded area, dropping
leaflets and announcing over loudspeakers that
everyone had better leave. As they passed through
checkpoints, the refugees would all be scrutinized,
some interrogated and detained, the rest given
shelter at a camp, set up, as I recall, by our State
Department. Then we'd bomb and shell the
vacated landscape, and when the dust had settled,
the allied troops would sweep across the peninsula, rounding up what was left of the 48th and
perhaps the 38th and their auxiliaries.

The plan had another preliminary feature. We
would distribute among our widely mistrusted
allies, the Army of the Republic of Vietnam, a set

of fake plans describing a large amphibious assault on the coast south of the peninsula. Decoy operations would begin down there, backing up the ruse. Only the ARVN division's commanding general would be told the real plan. The spies, presumably, would spread news of the fake plan, and the 48th Battalion might well take refuge in its stronghold, on the peninsula, just before the area was cordoned off.

I remember seeing many smiles in the briefing room that morning. The plan sounded clever. This was a big deal, besides. One General Cooksey would be in charge of the Army troops. It would be important for him to know the locations of the radios of the 38th VC Battalion and especially of the 48th. There would be no other likely way to know if the ruse had worked and the operation's main target was trapped. I would be the one who brought that information to the general.

I remember standing in front of the map back at my detachment, briefing my men—Schulzie, whom I had begun to try to train as Rosenthal's replacement, and Spikes, who had stood in for me at morning briefings during my R & R, and Pancho, who I knew would be interested. I said something like "We've got to be on our toes. This is a big deal."

They all seemed pleased. I think Pancho called

it a "shaky plan," and I think Spikes, too, gave it his highest praise and said, "**Decent**."

Soon our part of the operation had a name, Operation Russell Beach. The Marines' portion was called Bold Mariner. (Marine commanders thought it wise to keep their men in practice for amphibious assaults, but it was hard to tell how coming in by sea would gain them an advantage, unless soggy boots are an advantage.) At morning briefings, the operation seemed to be unfolding nicely. But without any help from me. Back at my detachment, I stood at the big map and stared at the yellow dot with the red eye. The last fix, from several days before, had put the 48th a little south of the Batangan Peninsula. Now, evidently, their radio had gone silent. This wasn't surprising. Probably the 48th had seen the beginnings of the phony amphibious assault south of the peninsula, and they were busy beating feet, as Pancho would say. Maybe they'd been fooled and were returning to Pinkville while our troops were advancing on them. Whatever **advancing** meant.

It was getting hard even to fantasize about what was really going on. Memories of training camp marches—of suffocating heat, of grooves of pain that the protruding metal parts of a machine gun made in the shoulders after only half a mile or so, of chafing at the crotch, of squatting over a hole in the ground, of the nauseating taste of water in a plastic canteen heated by the sun—all of that seemed very long ago. The game we used to play in the lounge, Diplomacy, felt as real to me. Standing at my map, waiting for the encrypted radio to crackle or the Teletype to clatter and deliver up the latest fix on the 48th Battalion, I was relieved of every other reality. But where was the 48th?

"Any news for us this morning, Lieutenant?" Colonel Chamberlain asked when I pulled the brown paper off the portable map in front of his chair at 6:00 A.M.

"No, sir. I'm sorry, sir. Not yet."

And then, suddenly, I had nothing to report to him, no information at all about any North Vietnamese or Vietcong unit. I got the word by Teletype from company headquarters. As I'd learned back at Fort Devens, in one of those classrooms with a bank-vault door, every sophisticated army periodically changes all its call signs, all the symbols its units use to identify themselves over the air. The NVA and VC had just changed theirs. Almost certainly this had nothing to do with Operation Russell Beach/Bold Mariner. They had done this before. It was predictable. But why, I wondered, did they have to choose this moment?

I drove to company headquarters in Chu Lai. I hardly knew the warrant officer who kept track of the enemy's communications network, the man who would now reconstruct that network. He was an old-timer. The gray in his hair was reassuring. I sat down in front of his desk. It was situated outside the door to the room where the ditty-bops listened through headphones to the enemy communications traffic.

So they'd changed everything around, and until he had the new network reconstructed, we wouldn't know where the 48th was. Did I have that right?

"That's an affirm."

But when would he have it reconstructed?

It was hard to say.

Boy, the sooner the better. He knew about Russell Beach. The heat was on.

He smiled.

Would we have the location of the 48th before our soldiers moved into their cordon?

His smile was friendly. He lifted his hands.

After you spend some time inside a bureaucracy, you develop strategies that turn into reflexes. The most reliable is flattery. I don't mean to say that this warrant officer, whose name I have forgotten, wasn't going to do his job however I behaved. But I had to be sure he'd hurry.

How in the name of this man's Army could he reconstruct a commo net anyway? I wondered. It wasn't as though I didn't feel sincerely curious.

He sat back in his swiveling desk chair. He lit

up a cigar, and hands behind his head, he allowed that, sure, his own role was complicated, but it was possible for him to play it only because of the skills of our ditty-bops over there in the next room. See, he said, every commo operator who taps out messages in Morse code does so in a way that is at least slightly different from that of every other commo operator. Our ditty-bops knew the distinctive sound of every enemy commo op's finger on the key, and the NVA and VC could change all their call signs and frequencies, but they couldn't change their commo operators, not many of them anyway.

When, scanning the airwaves, the ditty-bops who specialized in the 48th Battalion heard the telltale sound of its commo operator sending messages, and heard the new call sign attached to those messages, then it was a damn good bet that the 48th's radio had been found again. The warrant officer would need more than one such rediscovery, and other kinds of evidence, before he could put the map of the network back together. Progress would be slow at first. Then it would accelerate.

"Wow," I said.

He puffed on his cigar. This wasn't uninteresting, he allowed, and it was important for sure, American lives being at stake. But for sheer complexity and the fun of the chase, it couldn't compare to working on the interception of satellite communications. He was talking about a guy he'd once known at a listening post—was it in Turkey?—who could make a Russian satellite dump all its contents, when my mind began to wander. What would I tell Colonel Chamberlain? What would I tell General Cooksey? They'd be very disappointed.

Down on the Batangan Peninsula, I heard, the real operation was about to commence. The briefings that came before mine had a snap to them, a quick cadence. The map with the operation outlined on it looked like a real battle map, a map in a book of military history, with big red arrows depicting Stonewall Jackson's or Napoleon's cleverness. This was the kind of event professional soldiers waited for, and it seems to me it was one time when I sensed that fellow feeling in the briefing room included me. Anyway, no one called me the spot man that day, and a major moved a little sideways on the bench to make room for me. He even nodded to me. I imagined he might be thinking, Good to have you aboard. But my briefing didn't last long.

"Any news today, Lieutenant?"

"No, sir. Not yet."

In the afternoon I drove to Chu Lai again. I found the warrant officer bent over his desk, pencil in hand, papers scattered all around him.

Moments after I arrived, the door to the big room full of ditty-bops opened, and a tall young soldier in an olive-drab T-shirt appeared. A pair of earphones hung around his neck. He glanced at me, wearing a sour look. Maybe he remembered that message I'd sent some weeks back. "He's up," he said to the warrant officer and walked back inside the room of the ditty-bops. The warrant officer came right out of his chair and followed the ditty-bop.

"Do you think I'll have something on the 48th today?" I asked.

"Can't talk now," said the warrant officer.

I was staring at the map in our operations hootch that evening, considering a visit to the lounge. The cordon was going to be put in place with or without information from me. Who cared? I might as well give up and have a beer. The phone in the front room rang. It was the warrant officer. He said I'd be receiving a Teletype any minute.

"All right!" I said. "Outstanding!" I added. It wasn't something I'd usually do, use lifers' talk, but it sounded right.

I called the brigade intelligence officer. Was General Cooksey still at the briefing room? Could he wait a few minutes for me? I hovered over the shoulder of the commo op. I watched the Teletype keys scratch out the usual heading. First, the secret code word, SORTIE; it had been changed, maybe because of Pancho and me. Next the routing instructions, which I read, thinking, **Hurry up.** Then came the unit designation. It was indeed the 48th. Then the radius of the fix. Five hundred meters, the very best. Finally, the coordinates. I reached over and tore the sheet off the Teletype. There wasn't time to follow the new procedures and triple-wrap the piece of paper. I put in it my pocket and hustled out to the jeep. It was raining. I didn't even bother to put on my poncho.

Inside the briefing room, a small group of elderly men, elderly to me, stood at the map—the brigade S-2 and S-3, the new executive officer who had the necessary clearance, Colonel Chamberlain, General Cooksey. Perhaps it was the general's name that made me imagine him in a Confederate uniform. He was tall, and he had nice manners.

They all turned from the map when I came in the door. "Good evening, Lieutenant," said the general.

"Good evening, sir."

Colonel Chamberlain stood slightly off to one side. I felt a little pang, for feeling pleased that I was briefing a general instead of him.

"If I may, sir." I gestured toward the map.

"Certainly."

It was around 6:00 P.M., 1800 hours. I glanced

at the slip of paper, then quickly found the grid square on the map, then the exact spot within the square. Holding my finger on it—a spot right in the center of the Batangan Peninsula, a spot between the coast and the wall of soldiers even now moving into their cordon—I said, "Sir, at 1704 hours today, the 48th Main Force Battalion was located here."

The colonels and the general crowded in a little to look. Then the general turned to me with a big smile. He said, "We **got** 'em, Lieutenant!"

"Yes, sir!" I felt my own smile rising, like a blush.

ROUGHLY CONTEMPORANEOUS OFFICIAL MARINE documents say that Operation Bold Mariner/Russell Beach lasted from 13 January until 9 February 1969. They describe it as "the largest amphibious operation of the war." And they uniformly describe a happy ending:

> The total success of the action ashore far exceeds the enemy battlefield casualties. . . . A hitherto enemy sanctuary was surrounded without warning, then systematically searched and cleared, thereby once again serving the enemy notice no area is secure from the mobile striking

power of the forces of III MAF and the
Seventh Fleet. As a result of Operation
BOLD MARINER/RUSSELL BEACH, nearly
12,000 Vietnamese were returned to
GVN influence, after more than two
decades of VC control; 256 of them were
identified as VCI and taken into custody.

I can imagine having been assigned to write
that summary. The war was far from over then.
There were careers to be made. I'd have written
what my commanders wanted their commanders
to read, and for self-respect I might have made
these same small asides that I found in the once-
secret documents: "In retrospect, while the opportunity to meet and destroy in battle a large enemy
force did not materialize . . ." "The entire peninsula was found to be a labyrinth of cleverly con-
cealed tunnels, caves, and trenches . . ." "It is
quite possible sizable enemy forces used the exist-
ing tunnel network as an avenue to exfiltrate the
area." **The New York Times** reported on the operation, but not in any detail. It is hard to tell, from
the several articles in the **Times** and from the official, once-secret documents, exactly how many
people died. Perhaps only a dozen American soldiers, and God knows how many Vietnamese. In
any case, from what I heard at the TOC, the operation sounded like a failure.

Not surprisingly, once the cordon was estab-
lished, I got no further fixes on the 48th Battalion's radio, not for a long time. About a week after
the cordon began to sweep across the peninsula
toward the sea, I asked the S-3 if he thought the
48th had been destroyed. He seemed dubious. He
said our soldiers had found one cave containing
150 head of cattle. He did not think that we had
found every cave, or the majority of the 48th's
personnel and weapons.

Something like twelve thousand of the people
who had lived on the peninsula had left their
homes and land for the American-run refugee
camp outside the tightening cordon. I heard at
morning briefings that there was an outbreak of
dysentery among the refugees, and also that the
VC mortared the camp from time to time. Eventually, the Vietnamese went home, back to the
Batangan Peninsula. I'd never seen the place
myself, but an officer I'd met at the TOC had told
me that he'd often flown over it, and that it
looked lovely from the air, full of streams, ver-
dant with rice paddies and ordered hedgerows.
Obviously, the place looked different after the
operation, after the heavy shelling and the sor-
ties of B-52s, called "mini arc lites." I don't know
for sure exactly how different it looked, but a
few years after the war ended I did get a descrip-
tion from the writer Tim O'Brien. He was sta-

tioned on the peninsula after Operation Russell Beach. When he told me this, I remarked that the area of his base camp was said to be beautiful. "Beautiful?" he exclaimed. "It was all red earth!"

So that is what I imagine the refugees went home to once the operation ended. I have an article about their return, from the **Pacific Stars and Stripes,** quite descriptive in its way:

> BATANGAN PENINSULA, VIETNAM—The packs they carried were heavy, for they contained their life's belongings.
>
> Yet the refugees—women, children and a scattering of men—seemed not to feel the weight as they walked ashore on the Batangan Peninsula, returning to the one-time Communist stronghold 15 miles southeast of Chu Lai. . . .
>
> Almost 12,000 refugees began a 20-day exodus last month from the Combined Holding and Interrogation Center near Quang Ngai City back to Batangan in a massive resettlement project coordinated by the Quang Ngai Province chief. . . .
>
> Getting ready for the villagers' return required the clearing of four large vil-

lage sites and construction of a 25-mile road system by elements of the Americal Div.'s B Co., 26th Eng. Bn. . . .

To start the villagers anew, the South Vietnamese government provided each family with a "resettler's kit" comprised of carpentry tools, tin roofs and one month's supply of rice. . . .

By the time resettler's kits were being passed out, the excitement at headquarters was long past, and the old patterns of life had resumed, and on the map at my detachment, the dot like a red eye with a yellow rim was once again moving around the Batangan Peninsula.

I SIT IN THE BRIEFING ROOM, WAITING MY TURN, my mind drifting away on the droning voices. The captain from Artillery takes his place beside the map in front of Colonel Chamberlain, and, pointer stick in his right hand, glancing at a piece of paper in his left, he begins.

"Sir, we fired thirty rounds of HE Quick here, results unknown. And, sir, twenty-five rounds of HE Quick here, results unknown. And, sir . . ." I notice a change in his voice, an increase in its cadence, as in one mouthful he says, "One hundred twenty-three rounds of willy peter here, results seventy-five VC KIA. And, moving along, sir, thirty rounds of—"

"Wuh-wuh-wuh-wait a minute, Captain," says Colonel Chamberlain. "Guh-guh-go back to that one."

The artillery captain stiffens. "Yes, sir." He points again, again saying, "One hundred twenty-three rounds of willy peter here, sir. Results: seventy-five VC KIA."

Colonel Chamberlain rises from his chair. Bending over, he puts his finger on the spot on which all that white phosphorus rained down the night before. He studies it, then sits back and says to the artillery captain, "Tha-tha-**that's** a village, Captain."

"Yes, sir!" The captain stands at attention now, the last hiding place available to a soldier. I sympathize.

Colonel Chamberlain doesn't raise his voice. He stares at the captain. "That isn't a free-fire zone, Captain, is it?"

"No, sir."

"So wha-wha-what you mean is, two VC KIA and seh-seh-seventy-three women and children. Isn't that right, Captain?"

"Yes, sir."

The colonel folds his hands in his lap. He stares

at the captain. Then he says, very sternly for him, "Nuh-next time report it that way."

"Yes, sir."

Over months of morning briefings, I must have heard of many villages being bombed, both accidentally and on purpose, but it had been easy not to realize this. The reports were clinical and bland, the pointer jabbing at a spot I couldn't see on the map as the briefing officer read out the amount of ordnance expended. And no one in the audience had ever before made a translation. Looking back, I wonder if the colonel reported the embarrassing facts to his commanders at Division. I like to imagine that he did, and that this was the reason his own command ended after only four months. At the moment, I felt like applauding the colonel's candor, and I felt like running away.

The bombing of the village would have made a good subject for a letter to Sam or David, but I never mentioned it. "I was going to forget the war. I had made a separate peace," says Lieutenant Frederic Henry, the hero of **A Farewell to Arms**. On a night soon after the briefing that I was going to forget, I sat in my hootch and wrote to David:

> The war proceeds. We've exported all those things you spoke about, plus a substantial amount of misery. The one

thing that occurs to me is the justice of your remarks and speculation.

At last, though, there is something—"no, I don't want to do that or no, I won't think that"—most of my men have it and I am braver and more defiant than I thought I would be, and yet I still do my job.

I have a girlfriend in one of the villages, who is inscrutable but lovely. Sometimes we go there (it's off limits) and sit around and talk. She does my laundry. It's quieter there, too.

A huge storm is brewing over the mountains. I have all sorts of things to say but no time now and not quite the words. I hope that I could hate any man Oriental, Western or Venetian, or like one and all on similar grounds. The important thing is not to choose sides, because then you are at war, and I don't choose to be.

Evening is nigh.

Outside my hootch, the sky was clear and full of stars. I didn't have a Vietnamese girlfriend. I hadn't been to the ville in many months. I didn't mail the letter.

Sam wrote every week. Letters from him and

David meant a lot to me. I'd take them to my hootch, and even the thwacking of choppers, nearby and incessant, would recede. I'd be carried to a place where I felt I belonged, to the midst of the kind of conversation that seemed impossible here, conversation about literature and values, gentle and genteel. But I found the letters hard to answer.

I wanted to share my older friends' outrage at this war. At the same time, I wanted to suggest that I was more knowledgeable than they. I wanted to portray a rugged guy with smudges on his face from sleeping in a foxhole—one hand holding an M-16, the other resting protectively on the shoulder of a Vietnamese boy, named Go or Hanh. But I really did know some things they couldn't know, things I could not say. I knew how close you could get to this war—I was never more than a few miles away from a village being bombarded or a platoon caught in an ambush—and yet have it remain an abstraction, dots on a map. I also knew how to be confused.

I'd called myself "brave" and "defiant" in the unsent letter to David, finding words for exactly those qualities I thought I lacked. What would bravery and defiance look like here? Should I have described Colonel Chamberlain in my letters? I liked him. He was a decent, honest man. Did I expect **him** to stand up in that briefing the other day and say, "This war is wrong. We bombed a village by mistake, so I'm ordering an immediate halt in operations"?

Years later, when I traveled around the United States interviewing Vietnam combat veterans, I asked repeatedly what they thought they'd been fighting for. In Birmingham, Alabama, I spoke to a group of young African American men for whom, of course, no part of Vietnam had ever been an abstraction. One said, "We weren't fighting for anything. The war was only a way of making money for the civilians." Another said, "And to decrease the population of the United States." He added, "But we had a cause. Yeah, stay alive."

This was the commonest answer I heard from former combat soldiers. For myself, I think it might have sufficed if I'd been an infantry platoon leader. As it was, I felt, increasingly, that everything I did was worse than pointless. And still, perversely, I wanted the war, with all else it had to do, to lend my life some meaning.

CASSIUS

———⊟———

MY SUIT HAD ARRIVED FROM SINGAPORE. I'd ordered it imagining myself at a garden party in **The Great Gatsby.** It wasn't what I had expected—tight, pegged pants, narrow lapels, padded shoulders, a suit, I worried, fit for a bookie or a pimp. I wore it anyway on New Year's Eve in our lounge. When I woke up the next morning, I thought I remembered a contretemps with Pancho at the party, not the cause of the argument but only his saying to me before I staggered to my hootch, "Some people didn't grow up in a fucking mansion, Lieutenant." Maybe I only dreamed the incident. If not, he seemed by morning of the new year, 1969, to have forgiven or forgotten whatever I had said.

I was working at my desk in the operations hootch. It was a hot, fly-buzzing, dusty afternoon. I heard voices out in the front room, where the comsec guys worked—when they worked. I looked up and listened. The voices had a quality like a wrong smell in the house where you grew up and also a familiar quality that made me angry even before I placed it. Somebody, some person with an unfamiliar voice, was chewing out one of my men.

I walked to the doorway. The enlisted man sat at the comsec desk, his shoulders bent, as if beneath the weight of the person who stood over him, a young man fully dressed in fatigues with the brown bars of a second lieutenant on the points of his collar. He was a pudgy man, with the same quality that I saw in Colonel Riddle's face, faintly exuding that feeling of sinister weakness held together by starch, but in his case incipient, not fully formed, or maybe imagined. I'd met him recently, back at company headquarters in Chu Lai. He was a brand-new second lieutenant, in charge of comsec for the company. I stood in the doorway for a moment, listening.

"I expect better work from you, soldier. Keep goofing off and you'll be back in Chu Lai on KP."

The enlisted man, my man, was also fairly new in country, which was why he looked so cowed.

He had spotted me in the doorway and was looking at me sidelong, questioningly, I thought.

"Hey," I said.

The lieutenant turned, and he smiled. "Hey, Lieutenant Kidder. How you doin'?"

I smiled back. "Could you come in here a minute?"

The Teletype in the back room was rattling away. A couple of the commo ops were back there, talking. But the map room was empty. I lowered my voice. "What the fuck do you think you're doing?"

"Just doin' my job." My comsec men's output was grossly insufficient, he said.

"You got a problem with my men, you come to me," I said.

"I was just tryin' to help you out," he said.

The commo ops in the back room had stopped talking. Everyone in the operations hootch was listening, a sound all its own. I kept my voice low. "Don't you ever come out here and chew out **my** men. You understand?"

"Yes, sir."

We lieutenants didn't usually **sir** each other. How quickly I'd forgotten the way it felt to be a new guy. Was it memories of boarding school, how easy it was to be a successful bully, that made me want both to knock someone down and to help him up afterward? If comsec wasn't being done satisfactorily, I told the new lieutenant, I'd see that it was in the future. I walked him to his jeep. I clapped him on the shoulder as he climbed in beside his enlisted driver, who gave me a look behind the officer's back—a quick smile, a lifting of the eyebrows.

A few days later, on a routine trip to Chu Lai in the truck, just Schulzie and me in the cab, we passed an MP on Highway One.

"Hey, you! Put on your helmet!" the MP yelled at Schulzie.

Disciplinary orders from on high all seemed bizarre to me by then, pure malevolence toward soldiers.

"Stop the truck, Schulzie."

I put on my helmet and jumped out the door. I strode toward the MP, a young enlisted man. I must have looked fierce, because he came to attention.

"If you could see that my driver wasn't wearing his helmet, you could see that I'm an officer, and you should have saluted me," I said.

"Yes, sir." He saluted.

I saluted back, that crisp salute in which the flattened right hand is taken away from the forehead with a quick turn of the wrist.

Schulzie was grinning all the way to Chu Lai. "I guess you chewed his ass. I **guess**. Heeee."

At dawn a few days later, I trudged up the hill with my toilet kit on the path through tall grass. One night not long before, my men had gone to Chu Lai to see the new John Wayne movie about our war, **The Green Berets.** They had told me that the hundreds of GIs who were watching, in a grandstand outdoors, all started hooting and boo- ing and hissing when the movie showed a scene of ocean and the sun **setting** over it. I mounted the stoop of the operations hootch and paused a moment, looking toward the sunrise over the sea. Then I looked down at the table where I shaved. The gray basin was there as usual, but someone had already filled it with water. The commo op on duty came to the doorway. "I heated it up for you, Lieutenant. On the hot plate."

"Hey, thanks."

I understood the message. I was getting a lot of credit for a couple of small acts in defense of my men.

Later on that day, I was alone in operations with Rose, the commo op. You could always count on him not to keep a secret. "You know what the guys call you?" he asked me.

I made a face. I thought, Here we go again.

"Cassius," he said. "You know, like Cassius Clay?"

I didn't let him see me smile.

THE CONFIDENCE THAT CAME FROM WARM SHAV- ing water! Confidence bred certainty, which was always useful, as on the day when my one essential man, Spikes, came to me and said, "Lieutenant, they're sendin' us a nigger."

Racial strife, like combat, was an issue I hadn't had to deal with. The vast majority of young Americans sent to Vietnam and assigned to the combat arms came from the country's lower economic tiers, but a recruit with black or brown skin stood the greatest chance of being assigned to fight. The Defense Department's own statistics would later prove this. Black enlisted men made up about 8 percent of the armed forces and suffered about 15 percent of the casualties. But it was already obvious enough to everyone in Vietnam. There weren't many African Americans assigned to safe jobs like radio research. None were assigned to my detachment, and so it had been easy to ignore Spikes's habit of calling people in his drawl "Boy," then adding jocularly, "I don't mean Roy." I had never been to a civil rights demonstration, not even in the North. I knew only a few black Americans personally. But I knew I should be on their side. Without question, Sam and David would insist that I stick up for a black soldier under my command.

"Stoney," I said to Spikes, "you can't use that word again."

His jaw was set. I appealed to his sense of community. "This guy is going to be part of our detachment." I appealed to his patriotism, which I knew was strong. "He's an American just like us."

"Where's he gonna sleep?"

Pancho was sitting nearby. "He can sleep in my place."

Spikes shrugged. So far as I knew, he never mistreated the new guy. I think that after a week or so he actually thought of him as one of us. Melvin Harris. It would have been hard not to like him, even though he didn't drink. He was small and quiet and didn't shirk the communal chores. I think he believed first of all in staying alive. When he went outside our hootches, he always wore his steel pot, with the two chin straps dangling. I had several long talks with him, alone at night in operations when he was on duty. He told me a little of his past, a sad story of an alcoholic father in the slums of Philadelphia, a familiar story but one I'd never heard firsthand before. I remember arguing with him about the Black Panthers, who seemed menacing to me, and trying to get him to denounce them, but he wouldn't. Like Spikes, he seemed to feel he'd ended up in the wrong place, in his case because everyone else was white. He didn't want to be "Tomish," he'd say. He didn't want to be "a gray." But he fit in at my detachment. In my mind, I didn't shrink from taking most of the credit.

A MONTH OR SO AFTER SCHULZIE AND I HAD returned from Singapore, A truck, a deuce and a

half, pulled into our parking area. As usual I went to
the front of operations to check out the visitors.
They were soldiers from the radio research detachment up north on LZ Baldy. They'd just come back
from R & R, one of my men told me. I lingered
there, watching, because something seemed to be
going on. An enlisted man, heading back to Baldy,
was standing in the open bed of the truck, leaning
down and speaking to Schulzie. I couldn't hear what
he was saying. Then Schulzie was walking back
toward the enlisted hootches, with his head down.

Well, my men had their secrets. I wouldn't
intrude. I went back to the map room. Another
hot day dragged by. "Where's Schulzie?" I asked
when, as was usual now, we met up and walked
together to the H-Troop mess hall for dinner.

"Ahhh, he's shaky today," said Pancho. For
once, he seemed to use the word literally.

I had a clear sense that night that I should avoid
the lounge. I could hear voices coming through
the screen walls, and some anguished-sounding
yelling. I went to my hootch. I was lying on my
cot, reading, on the olive-drab poncho liner, under
the olive-drab mosquito net, when I heard a knock
on the door. Schulzie, slurring his words, asked,
"Mind if I come in, Tracy?"

"Sure." I felt reflexively uncomfortable. A
drunken soldier in my hootch, calling me by my
first name. We weren't in Singapore.

Schulzie sat down on my footlocker. "She's still working," he said. "A friend of Pancho's was in Singapore, and he found out she's still working."

"Who?" I said. "Oh, yeah. Jesus, Schulzie, I'm sorry." I thought of saying but didn't, "Well, she's a whore, Schulzie. I mean, they have to live, too."

"And I sent her money so she wouldn't have to work."

"Oh, God, that makes it worse." I put some indignation in my voice. "Fucking women, you know, Schulzie." Then I asked, "You sent her money? How much did you send her?"

He didn't want to say exactly. Hundreds anyway, that was clear.

I let him talk. I didn't have much choice. I kept thinking I could understand his feelings if the girl in question weren't a whore, or were at least good-looking. It was a hot night, murmurings of insects punctuated now and then by thumps from the mortars nearby. He sat with his head bowed, his barrel chest bare. "I don't know what to do."

"I don't think you should send her any more money, Schulzie. She's a whore."

"I know! I know she's a fucking whore! I know."

"And she's still working."

"But, see, this is the thing." Suddenly, he was crying. "I don't care. I still love her."

It felt odd to be on the other side of such a conversation. I felt like telling him to forget it. She looked too much like a chicken to worry about, and besides, she was clearly not a person of good character. But I felt I owed him sympathy. I felt I owed all disappointed lovers sympathy, being one of the brotherhood.

"I don't care! I still love her." He had stopped crying. He looked up at me. "The thing is, I'm worried it won't work out."

"I think you're right, Schulzie."

"I don't care what my parents would think."

"Think they'd disapprove?"

"If I brought her home for a wife? Yeah, they wouldn't like it."

"You mean because she was a whore?"

"No, 'cause she's a zip. I don't care what they'd think. But the thing is, see, I'm afraid it might hurt my chances of becoming governor of Alaska."

I remember feeling so surprised I almost laughed, and then I wasn't tempted. Schulzie had told me he'd visited Alaska once, and that he loved the wide-open feeling it gave him, and that he planned to go back there when he got out of the service. I hadn't taken him very seriously. Lately, though, I had been writing in my letters that I was going to buy a boat and sail around the world. I hadn't worked out the finances yet, but it seemed important to have a dream like that. "I didn't know you wanted to be governor of Alaska," I said.

He was rolling his shoulders from side to side, hands clasped, head down. "I know it sounds fucking stupid."

"No, no. It doesn't sound stupid."

"What do you think I should do?"

"I don't know, Schulzie. I don't know if it really would hurt your chances of being governor, but if you've been sending her money, and she's still working . . ."

"But I forgive her!"

This went on for a while. Finally, I told him, "I think you should go to bed. You'll feel better tomorrow. Anyway, I've got to go to sleep now."

He stumbled out the door, thanking me profusely.

I didn't see much of him the next day, because he was sleeping it off. The other men covered for him. The day after that I saw him moping around, grumbling when the others tried to talk to him. It seemed very important to me that I find a way to cheer him up. I'm not sure why. Maybe because I could imagine his unhappiness. But I knew that feeling of something warm gone out of your life, the thing you hung on to, more an idea than a fact, when people yelled at you or you were wishing you were anywhere but in this place or on this training camp march or in this infernal Army

kitchen, sergeants shouting, Sounds like a personal problem to me! I understood. I was glad I
wasn't the only one. Then I had an idea.

I went to work in my hootch right after lunch.
I wrote to Schulzie's girl in Singapore:

> I am sorry to have to write to tell you
> bad news. I knew your fiancé Schulzie
> well. I was his platoon leader. Yesterday
> while we were out on patrol, he was
> gravely wounded. He was trying to save
> the lives of his comrades, and he
> jumped on a live hand grenade that
> would have killed us all. Before he died,
> your name was on his lips, and he gave
> me two hundred dollars, and he asked
> me to send it to you. But lately my
> grandmother has been very sick and my
> cousin, too, and I knew from what
> Schulzie said about you that you would
> understand.

I went looking for Schulzie and gave him the
letter. "I don't know, it's just something that came
to me. You can use it if you want to."

His eyes widened as he read, and for a moment
I thought I'd made a mistake. Then he yelled,
"This is great! This is fuckin' great!" He laughed,
head back, arms opened to the sky. He ran off

carrying the letter, to show it to the other men. A little later, he came back wondering if we could rewrite the part about the hand grenade and make it a Bouncing Betty mine. I think Bouncing Betty mines figured now and then in episodes of **Combat!**

The next day I saw Schulzie walking around the compound with his shirt off and his arms raised in the air, as if someone invisible were holding a gun to his back and marching him over to the vehicles, marching him into the lounge, marching him up to the operations hootch. The other men just shrugged and walked around him. Finally I went out and said, "Schulzie, what are you doing?"

He gave me a sly grin. "I'm Chicken Little and the sky is falling."

If someone had told me I could leave for Fort Home tomorrow, I would have packed at once. But I realized I was as close to happy as I'd ever been in uniform. My job was like all jobs; succeeding at it made it a better job. I still wasn't sure how I ought to feel about what I was doing here, or whether I ought, ought morally, to be here at all. But my shaving water was warm in the mornings, and the prospect of seeing the stuttering colonel each day made me feel less responsible for whatever might be wrong about the job I was doing. Schulzie never mentioned the whore from

Singapore again. He had a resilience that I should have envied.

SOME MONTHS BACK, WHEN I STILL WENT ON swimming trips, my men and I had arrived at the beach and found a bunch of GIs already on the shore, in the midst of strange work. They had driven half a dozen Army trucks onto the hard-packed sand, right up to the lapping waves, and were washing the trucks in salt water, shirts off and whooping.

The scene had stuck with me. I remembered Spikes saying those guys were morons. But American boys aren't usually stupid about trucks. More likely, it now seemed to me, they had a commander who cared at least as much about appearances as about functionality, the kind of commander who would threaten to punish his men for driving dirty trucks and ignore the fact that to drive a truck ten feet around a place like LZ Bayonet was to cover it with a fine orange dust. I imagined, that is, that those men had a commander like our Colonel Riddle, and that they had said to one another as they'd headed for the beach, "He wants the vehicles washed again? We'll fuckin' wash his vehicles."

Our own three-quarter-ton truck had broken down, and the lieutenant who ran our company's

motor pool in Chu Lai had sent us another. I
didn't trust that lieutenant. He had red hair and a
choleric-looking, perpetually sunburned face, and
I thought he enjoyed haranguing EM. I suspected
that he disliked me, and I wasn't very surprised
when I saw the replacement truck he sent us. It
ran well enough, but it was battered.

I made an inventory of all its dents and rust
spots, a list two pages long, then typed the list in a
memo, which I sent to my captain in Chu Lai. I
kept the carbon copy for myself. Cover-your-ass
memos were the kinds of things that small-minded
lifers spent their best energies writing. But I had a
feeling the dented truck might become a problem
for me. I suppose an infantry platoon leader, a sur-
vivor of that much harder test, would also have
refined premonitions into instincts.

A week or two later, some of my men drove our
homely truck to Chu Lai on the very day when
Colonel Riddle happened to be visiting the company headquarters. The colonel was being given a
tour by the motor pool lieutenant, the one who
had sent us the battered-looking truck. According
to my men, the lieutenant spotted our deuce and
a half and brought the colonel over to have a look,
telling him that this disgraceful vehicle came from
my detachment. Maybe the colonel was giving
him a hard time and he was trying to deflect the
criticism. Who knew? Who cared?

I had recently begun a fitness program, with Schulzie as my trainer. He didn't work out himself—he just shouted encouragement. I wanted to be looking strong and fit a few months from now, when I'd go home and choose not to see Mary Anne. The landline phone rang in the midst of my push-ups. It was Colonel Riddle himself.

"Lieutenant Kidder, you busy right now?" His voice sounded friendly, too friendly.

"No, sir, I'm just getting some exercise." One recent directive from Saigon stressed the importance of getting exercise, so this seemed like a safe thing to say.

"Well, you get some exercise on this truck of yours!" he shouted. I had to hold the receiver away from my ear. "You get yo'self here to Chu Lai right now!"

"Yes, sir!"

I was turning in at the division's main gate, with my memo in a folder on the seat beside me, when a jeep coming the other way pulled up. It was my captain, the company commander, that reasonable man. He looked harried. "Go back," he said. "I have your memo. I've taken care of it."

There seemed to be no end of ways to get in trouble. For instance, the story I'd heard about some colonel who, faced with a big inspection, discovered he had one more tank than authorized and in desperation drove it himself into a lake. He was found out, of course, and was spending the rest of his life paying for the tank. I heard that story twice from different people. Perhaps it was apocryphal. But it sounded plausible to me. A couple of months before, I myself had realized we possessed far more ammunition than we were supposed to. I'd imagined some field grade officer coming to inspect us and toting up our armaments. So I had buried the excess ammo here and there on the little wooded hill beside operations. Then the officer in charge of security on LZ Bayonet had come around to tell me that they were going to burn all wooded areas inside the perimeter and our hill was on his list. I imagined the buried ammo and hand grenades exploding and killing the soldiers who were setting fire to the brush. I warned the officer that the old-timers in my detachment remembered people burying ammo on that hill before I took command. The officer looked hard at me. I shrugged. But I'd passed the responsibility for accidents to him. I knew he wouldn't burn the hill.

Inspections still worried me. But they were like those dangerous intersections where people rarely get in accidents because they are forewarned. I'd learned a way to keep commanders happy and my men from losing faith in me. Once every month or two, Chu Lai would let me know that a field grade officer from some higher head-quarters of Radio Research planned to visit us. I'd stand at the bar in our lounge and give the men the news. We had to do some cleaning up, I'd say. Pancho would usually protest. "What are they gonna do to us, Lieutenant? Send us to Viet-nam?" Another man might say, "We're fuckin' at war and these lifers want our fuckin' boots spit-fucking-shined?"

But I had some real authority with them now, even, it seemed, with Pancho, and in the end they would surrender to my logic, the same I'd long used, with mixed success, to inveigle Pancho to the barber. If a colonel or general came out here and didn't like what he saw, there'd be no end of inspections by captains and majors. All we had to do to avoid that was to disrupt our routines for a day at most and prepare for the lifer's visit. We would clean up the vehicles, sweep the dust out of the operations hootch, maybe oil its plywood floor, and make sure that, when the brass arrived, everyone was in full uniform and hard at work. The lifer would take a quick look around, I'd brief him at the big map about the local tactical situa-tion, maybe take him up to the TOC and intro-duce him to the S-2 and S-3, and he would depart, congratulating himself on having such a fine detachment within his command. In my mind, we were washing trucks in salt water. It had worked so far.

It was March. Colonel Chamberlain's turn at commanding the brigade had ended less than a week before. There hadn't been time or occasion yet for me to get to know the new colonel or his staff. I didn't care if I never did. I could look at my calendar now and see big X's covering two-thirds of my allotted days, consigning them to memories, including some, from the time of the stuttering colonel, that I thought I'd be happy to repossess. Looking back, these many years later, at the letters I had been writing home for a month or so, I notice the same old references to drinking heavily and Vietnamese girlfriends and children I was befriending in the ville and imaginary threats of enemy offensives. The Jazz Age diction remained. I was going to sail around the world. But the tone is different in all of them. I actually wrote in one letter, "I've had a good two months."

I wasn't very worried when my captain called from Chu Lai to say we should expect a visitor from Nha Trang, one Major Great. Odd name, I thought. An ASA general was coming to visit Chu Lai in a couple of weeks. This Major Great would look us over first, in order to make sure that

Colonel Riddle would look good in the event the general chose to visit my detachment.

We made the usual preparations. The major came at a civilized hour, around ten in the morning. When he arrived, in a jeep—stirring up dust that would, of course, settle on the freshly oiled floors of our operations hootch—we had the scenery arranged. Even the men off duty were filling new sandbags. I came out to the parking area. He was just another field grade officer, with an oak leaf on his collar, about my height, wearing a helmet, always faintly ridiculous-looking when combined with starched combat fatigues. I thought I saw hints of gray in the close-cropped sidewalls around his ears. Maybe a little old for his rank, I thought.

I snapped up a salute, which he returned. He offered his hand. I shook it firmly. He smiled. He smiled as I took him through the gate in the barbed-wire enclosure surrounding the operations hootch, as I showed him the comsec man busy monitoring brigade frequencies and the commo op at the Teletype and our burn bag in place for destroying classified information. I described the system that my intemperate message back to Chu Lai months ago had inspired. "And, Major Great, sir, we now get most of our fixes by radio, directly from the planes, which means we can get the information to Brigade much more quickly." I didn't mention that there were days when we couldn't get the radio to work.

"Looks good, Lieutenant," he said, still smiling. "Now let's take a look at your men's quarters."

The men's quarters? No one ever had inspected those hootches before. I was trying to think. **"Could you come back in a few hours, sir?"** Did I say that aloud? Could he read my thoughts? "Yes, sir," I said.

I'd spent parts of every evening before bed in our lounge, but I couldn't remember the last time I'd been inside the men's hootches. In the first one we inspected, clotheslines were strung from the ceiling, T-shirts drying on them. A few jungle boots and Ho Chi Minh sandals were out of place. Footlockers stood open with clothes and toilet gear all jumbled inside. That morning most of my men hadn't made their beds—hadn't pulled the poncho liners that served as sheets neatly over their cots, maybe because they'd been busy getting operations ready.

It didn't look half as messy as I'd feared, but a face was pushing itself close to my face. The major did not raise his voice. It sounded all the more vehement for that. "This is a disgrace, Lieutenant."

The next hootch looked about the same. He stared at the area Pancho had partitioned off and now shared with Harris. I held my breath. Where was the green gun? The blowtorch? The other unauthorized treasure that he'd collected and that I didn't know about? But there was nothing in sight, just an unmade cot and slight disarray. The hootches didn't look like stateside barracks, every soap dish and toothbrush in the same place in every footlocker, every bed made up so tightly you could bounce a quarter off the blankets, but they weren't nearly as messy as most normal people's bedrooms. No messier than my own hootch, I realized, and then I thought: Oh, God.

I followed Major Great outside. "Your men are living like pigs, Lieutenant Kidder. How do you explain this?" He wasn't barking at me. He sounded sincerely surprised. This didn't sound like a question. I didn't think I should answer.

"Well, Lieutenant?"

"No explanation, sir."

"All right. I want all of your men out here, except for the ones doing essential work."

"Yes, sir." I turned to Spikes, who had been following us at a little distance. "Sergeant Spikes, get the men out here. Now."

"Yessir."

Spikes snarled at the men. I knew he was trying to help me. He got them in a line in front of the enlisted hootches, all except for the comsec man and commo op on duty. Five men and a sergeant standing at attention in a line on the path of bare ground that ran between the hootches and the small wooded hill with our antennas on top and the buried ammo. The path led to the bunkers and the men's shitter. At least Major Great hadn't inspected the shitter.

The major walked slowly down the line, examining each man. With me at his side. He didn't talk to them. He talked to me about them. "This man needs a haircut."

"Yes, sir."

"Your sergeant's boots are unacceptable, Lieutenant."

I looked down at Spikes's boots. They weren't very well shined. But at least he wasn't wearing his completely unshined ones.

Major Great stopped in front of Pancho. "Look at this man's uniform, Lieutenant."

I had been worrying about Pancho's hair, which once again looked a little long. Now I was worrying about Pancho. He was looking squarely at the major, but with his head cocked slightly to one side. The other men looked frightened. Pancho looked both curious and irritated.

"There are holes in this man's uniform, Lieutenant," Major Great said.

"That's right, sir," said Pancho. "That's because the zips who do our laundry rub them on rocks in the river."

Major Great didn't look at Pancho's face. It was

a tactic, I realized in the functioning part of my mind. A field grade officer could pretend he didn't even notice certain soldiers. The major spoke only to me. "Tell that man to get a new uniform," he said and moved on down the line.

He told me to dismiss the men. Then he said he wanted to talk to people I worked with on the brigade staff. So I drove him up to the TOC in our jeep, driving very carefully, while Major Great spoke to me in that same calm voice, saying, "I'm really amazed at the way you run your detachment, Lieutenant. I'm trying to think what I should do."

I introduced Major Great to the major in charge of brigade intelligence, the S-2, seated at his desk inside the big bunker. While I stood beside him, Major Great said, in a calm but now ingratiating voice, "I want to check on Lieutenant Kidder's performance."

The S-2 shrugged. "I've only been here a few days, Major. I really can't say."

If only Colonel Chamberlain were still here, I thought. He and his staff would have put in a good word for me.

I drove Major Great back to my detachment. He got out. I stood beside him. He was gazing down the hill at my hootch. "Are those your quarters?"

"Yes, sir."

He began to step forward, then stopped. A hand went to his chin. "No, that isn't necessary," he said. He turned to me. "I'm not sure what I'm going to do, Lieutenant Kidder. When do you give your briefing tomorrow?"

"Zero six hundred, sir."

He brought his face closer to mine, too close, crossing with impunity the boundary of respect. Getting in your face—I felt as if his was trying to get inside mine. Looking back at his, I saw a picture that generalized itself: the pores in the skin, the stubs of whiskers closely shaved but beginning to grow, a pair of eyes to size me up, a mouth to chew me out. It was the face of this system in which a person only two ranks above me had ineffable power—to make trouble over trivia, to make me feel weak, even to wreck my delicate relations with my men. The lieutenant of my letters would have handled this situation with supreme indifference. I had thought I was catching up to him. I had thought that any day now I really might be him. But I could feel us parting ways. It was as if I looked around and couldn't find him.

Staring at the face that was staring at me, I recoiled inwardly, but I didn't move.

"I have to think about what I should do, Lieutenant Kidder," Major Great was saying calmly. "I'll be back out here at zero eight hundred tomorrow. I expect to see a vast improvement by then."

"Yes, sir." He was waiting, I realized. I saluted.

He returned the salute. I stood there watching him drive off. The men started gathering around me.

"Fuckin' puke!"

"Kiss my ass, motherfucker!"

"Hey, Lieutenant, do you **believe** that shit?"

Pancho was scowling. "Flatdick."

Down in my hootch some days later, I made notes for a new story:

> There was a Major Great who used to come in a helicopter, raising dust, spreading it through the screen walls, and climb on things, saying, "This hootch is dusty," who found a spiderweb in the barrel of Melvin Harris's rifle. Then Pancho, dark glasses, black hair on the forehead, comes out with his illegal captured weapon, green, insectlike gun. He saunters up to the openmouthed Major Great and says, "Hee hee hee." "You begged your last beg, sir," I say. Pancho sticks the Swedish K in Major Great's open mouth and blasts him. We cut him up in little pieces, put them in cement we have ready, make small blocks, then take them in the truck to the South China Sea and drown them.

What I actually said to the gathered men was: "Look, we've got to clean up this place. We've got to hurry. He's coming back tomorrow morning."

I took Spikes aside. "Can you help me? Please." His jaw muscles flexed. He wouldn't quite look at me. But what did I care at that moment?

"Okay, Lieutenant."

Major Great wasn't going to inspect my hootch. I could work with the men on theirs. I helped one arrange his footlocker, I helped another take down the laundry lines. The men went along with the cleanup, even Pancho, though he didn't speak to me. He was straightening up his footlocker, muttering to himself, as I passed through his area, and I realized I shouldn't feel panicked, but the thought only made me feel more panicked. In one of the men's hootches, I spotted a pair of unpolished boots on the floor beside a cot. I grabbed them, took them down to my hootch, and polished them, along with my own. I hurried back to the men's hootches with a broom. Spikes was rolling up the canvas flaps that covered the hootches' screen walls and tying them neatly in place, so that they looked almost like curtains. Nice touch, I thought as I hurried by.

We finished around midnight. I drank four or five beers in the lounge and went down to my hootch. I climbed into my cot and suddenly, to my surprise, I was weeping. I'm just exhausted, I thought. Could anyone hear me? I went on crying quietly, and then little by little I gave myself to it. Aware that the sounds might be wafting out of my hootch but not caring, almost enjoying myself—oh, in a way, this feels good—I cried myself, quite literally, to sleep.

I was up a few hours later. I went to the colonel's briefing and returned, feeling frantic again. I found Pancho outside. "He's coming soon," I said.

Pancho had a disgusted look on his face. He muttered something, walking away. I thought I heard the words "Ain't like a man."

Major Great looked very fresh in his fatigues. He made a quick tour of the men's quarters. "This is fine, Lieutenant." Was that all? I thought. Just "fine"? After what I'd been through? But I felt a great relief, almost like happiness when, before climbing into his jeep, he said, "If you keep your detachment in this kind of condition, Lieutenant, you won't have any problems."

And then I went down to my hootch, lay down on my cot, turned on my fan, pulled the mosquito net around me, always that smell of treated rope, that Army-surplus-store smell, and fell asleep again. I slept through the baking heat. When I woke up it was evening.

Oh, no, I thought. What did I do last night? What did they hear? What had Pancho said? Had he really said, "Ain't like a man"?

When I walked into the lounge, they were all shirtless and drinking, and they stopped talking, and most of them didn't quite look at me. Schulzie came up and gave me a friendly punch on the arm. "Have a beer, Lieutenant."

I felt sick, all hollowed out. I sat down and took a long swig of beer, the usual Carling Black Label in the rusty cans, but at the first contact bitter and bracingly fizzy. Watching myself stroke the beer can, I told them I hated the Army as much as they did. I didn't believe that officers' shit didn't smell. I was going to serve out my time here because I had no choice, and I'd do whatever I could to keep the lifers from puking on them. And from now on, they should call me by my first name.

The men looked at one another. A couple of them smiled, a couple shrugged.

"Good by me," Spikes said. He looked serious.

Pancho was standing at the end of our makeshift bar. He said, "Nah, fuck that. I'll just call you Lieutenant."

I went back to my hootch. I didn't sleep much. Clearly, Pancho knew my secret. So did the other men, probably. If only it had to do with cowardice of the rational, physical kind, and not with what my favorite writers called "character." It seemed more important than anything, and I didn't believe I would get another chance to prove I had it, the way Conrad's Lord Jim does. I was aware my reaction was excessive, and I think I sensed the cause. If only I didn't have such an inflated idea of myself, then I wouldn't have been afraid of some major with a funny name, and I wouldn't have made a spectacle of myself in front of the men, and I wouldn't be lying in my cot, knowing that the memories of the last two days would be coming home with me.

THE DEATH OF
LIEUTENANT DEMPSEY

—■—

A YEAR LATER, I IMAGINED LIEUTENANT Dempsey's long last day.

He has been through a great deal by now. He's gotten his platoon lost. His men have killed a water buffalo and terrorized an elderly peasant. On the second day on combat patrol, he awakes in his foxhole with firm resolution:

> The old water buffalo must never be killed again, nor old men beaten with stones. Pride jumped up and danced in him. "I'm in control here, I'm in control," he sang to himself as he ran for-

ward from the rear, as he supervised
the order of march. He made up a song
to the tune of "Jody" and sang it as he
ran along in cadence, singing, "Jody,
Jody, don't be blue. We are fighting for
Vietnamese, too. Jody, Jody, don't be
sad. Second platoon's best platoon in
the whole damn land." It was a tune
they used to sing while marching in
ROTC summer camp. Only these words
were his own. And he was singing
under his breath, trotting along in the
airborne shuffle and looking at the
troops. . . .

But then he realizes the men are mocking him.
He descends into a rage. He loses all control of his
platoon. By midday, his men are gang-raping the
Vietnamese girl and the sergeant is about to take
his turn. Dempsey tries to intervene. He orders
the sergeant to stop, the sergeant disobeys, and
Dempsey announces that the sergeant is under
arrest. The platoon slogs on.

And that is how they came into the
province of the hills, where a troubling
vaporous smell came down from the
jungle and met them. Then the land
behind them turned up its evening

mellowness. And then, there before them, among a stand of trees with narrow trunks and leaves like African hair, of yellow, green, and purple bushes, they first caught sight of a ruined building.

This was the place where the story ends. Here they stopped walking and hushed awhile and stared at the ruin through the trees. Then this was the time of Ivory Fields.

Dempsey takes up residence alone in the ruin. "In what little light remained, Dempsey now finished brushing off his pack and did a little careless whistling. Why should he care? Nobody was anybody else's business." He neatens up his gear.

Long, bony fingers arranged these things and were arranging when he began to cry.

It was what he had been waiting for.

Convulsed and twitching like some wounded animal, and long-legged as a spider, Dempsey laid himself on his back and wept into his hands. His lips parted in the dark, his teeth appeared. He was leaping up. He was meeting the night sky, fighting, twisting. It was exquisite pain. Some stars were out already, but through the trees now all rushed out, like very eager things. Darkness flooded the air. But soon the tropic night was only muttering again and was as sweet as the tropics around him. And the stars winked warm and brightly like little silver fishes swimming over him, tickling him and consuming. Hid in full darkness, the awkward young man lay with his guns and his flashlight beside him, a warrior of sorts.

Actually, he is about to be a warrior for the first and only time. The sergeant has arranged a misunderstanding between the lieutenant and Ivory Fields, so that each believes the other intends to rape the girl, as the rest of the men already have. The moment will be Dempsey's next to last on earth.

Hawklike face forward, Lieutenant Dempsey sang out delighted into the dark. "I'm protecting her!" He heard his rival bellow again, and his own delighted yell back at him, but the next things he heard were not like sounds at all but thuds the soft parts of his body

heard. That was all right. His pain was
not a moment long, and was white.

A FEW DAYS AFTER MAJOR GREAT'S VISIT, I ASKED
Spikes if he thought burning the shit in my latrine
was something I shouldn't make the men do. He
paused, looking me in the eyes, and then he said
that no, it wasn't too much to ask. A few days
later, I was taking my morning nap when I heard
Pancho outside yelling that my shitter was burning. I grabbed the fire extinguisher that sat by the
door of my hootch, but it made just one feeble
squirt. Pancho said he guessed he'd used too much
diesel fuel. Since then, I'd used the enlisted men's
latrine.

On a day soon afterward, I was looking out
the screen walls of operations, and I saw Melvin
Harris sitting in the passenger seat of the three-
quarter-ton truck, helmet on, chin straps dangling. He looked unhappy. Pancho had that green
gun of his slung over his shoulder. He handed
Harris the dog, Tramp, and then climbed into the
driver's seat. For days beforehand Pancho had
been saying the animal was sick. It just seemed to
have a cold, I'd told him. But Pancho had insisted,
"No, he's sick." I remembered it as a puppy walking along behind Pancho, wagging its tail. Lately,

Pancho had been shaking his head, looking back at the now half-grown dog, saying, "You're sick, Tramp. You're fuckin' sick." I wasn't surprised when he and Harris came back without Tramp. When we were alone in operations that night, Harris said to me, "It was so **sad.** That nice little dog. I don't know why he had to shoot that dog."

I said only, "Well, it was his dog."

What I liked about Pancho was all wrapped up in what I didn't like or was afraid of. At times like that, I saw him as unfathomable, and unstoppable. Certainly it was easier to see him that way, but I wished I'd tried to reason with him about the dog the way I did about haircuts and inspections. I couldn't help but wonder if he just wanted to try out his green gun on something living. Now that he had tried it out, he packed it up for home. He'd learned that what held for stereos was also true of refrigerators. A soldier could buy a refrigerator over here and ship it home. So he'd bought a refrigerator at the Chu Lai PX. He'd taken the back off it, dismantled the Swedish K, secreted the pieces of the gun among the refrigerator's innards, put the refrigerator back together, and shipped it to Fort Home.

Not long after all of that, two weeks or so after Major Great's visit, Pancho got permission to leave my detachment for the radio research detachment at LZ Baldy, some thirty-five miles to the north. It seemed amazing to me that a lowly enlisted man could get himself transferred so easily and quickly, but in Pancho's case it made sense. I figured the authorities in Chu Lai were happy to have him as far away as possible. He told me, "I'm gonna beat feet, Lieutenant." I said I was sorry he was leaving, meaning more than I said. He told me, "I'm too short for this shit, Lieutenant. Too many fucking pukes coming out here. I'm gonna go hide at Baldy." He had friends there. They didn't get inspected as often as we did.

For traveling, everyone had a standard-issue olive-drab duffel bag. Except for Pancho, who packed his gear in a red mailbag he'd picked up somewhere. I watched him toss it up into the truck that was driving him away. I felt more bereft than I'd ever felt at the departure of a friend. From now on my detachment would be lacking versatility. More than that, I suspected he was leaving, at least in part, to get away from me, the disappointing spectacle of me.

I saw him briefly a week or so later. In the wake of Major Great, I'd decided we had too many hootches to take care of and should dismantle one. My captain in Chu Lai approved but said, "The roof belongs to this company. I want that roof." Technically, it belonged to LZ Bayonet, to the brigade. But the captain wanted another hootch built for the detachment at LZ Baldy, and metal roofing material was hard to come by. A job for Pancho, clearly. He and a bunch of other soldiers from Baldy came and scalped it off in no time, Pancho bossing the operation. They covered it with tarps in the back of their truck and got away.

A couple of weeks after that, I heard some news about him. Pancho had told me that whenever he went to Chu Lai he would look around for the operations officer, would yell hello to him, and give him his shaky "Heh-heh-heh-sir" laugh. Pancho had told me once, "That lieutenant's shaky, he never fucks with me." Now, visiting company headquarters in Chu Lai, I stopped in at the office of the operations officer, and the first subject he mentioned was Pancho. "I heard he shot his dog."

"Well, he said the dog was sick."

The lieutenant put his hands flat on his desk, as if he were going to stand up in a hurry. "But he just couldn't wait to do it, could he?"

Then the lieutenant looked around, as if afraid someone might overhear, and said in a low voice, "Do you know what he did up at Baldy?"

"No." I was sincerely curious.

"He threatened to put a poisonous snake in Lieutenant Johnson's bunk!"

I didn't know Lieutenant Johnson well, but I liked him. I said that Pancho was probably joking. I wondered. It wasn't like Pancho to make outright threats. I imagined that Lieutenant Johnson told him to get a haircut, and Pancho replied that people who puked on EM scum some-fucking-times found bamboo vipers in their racks. Anyway, Pancho wasn't my problem anymore.

I had come to Chu Lai that day to ask my company commander if I could spend the rest of my time doing some job at headquarters and have another lieutenant replace me at the detachment. But the only lieutenant who might have been available had tried some time ago to trade jobs with me, and I had turned him down. Now his situation had improved, and he demurred. My captain sent out his second in command to have a talk with me. We sat in my detachment's hillside bunker, looking west at the steep hills. He asked me what was wrong. I liked the man, but I could hardly begin to explain. I told him I was just tired, but I'd be all right, and I didn't mind finishing my time out here. I turned away as I said this, averting my eyes, gazing again at the hills. They'd been transformed some time back, when planes had swooped down dropping trails of the defoliant Agent Orange all around the base camp. I couldn't remember the date, only that it had been the worst-smelling day of my life. The leaves hadn't fallen yet but had simply turned a sickly orange.

I really was tired. Sergeant Spikes had decided

to stay in country an extra six months. In return, he got a thirty-day leave to the States. I'd refused my commander's offer of a new sergeant, saying I could manage until Spikes returned. I didn't mind the extra work, but now, really for the first time, I was responsible for an enlisted man whom I despised. Higgins. He was tall, with stooped shoulders, always trying to get out of the communal chores, and if he got his way and someone did his chores for him, he'd say in a whining southern accent: "I was about to do that. How come y'all didn't wait for me?"

Several times the MPs caught Higgins and one of the other men in the whorehouse in the ville. Higgins always managed to get someone like Rose caught, too. After the first of those arrests, the base camp's provost marshal, its chief cop, another major, told me he wanted a written report of the disciplinary action I was going to take. So I had to type up reports that made it sound as if I had punished my men.

I didn't much mind the deceptive paperwork. I was good at it by now. But I disliked going into the brigade stockade and retrieving Higgins and whoever else was locked up with him. I'd wear a disgusted look for the desk sergeant. I'd say, "These men, always out to mess with us, huh, Sarge?" The problem was that I had begun to believe it. And the place itself gave me the creeps.

It was a shack, essentially, with makeshift wooden doors to its two jail cells.

I was standing there one evening, signing papers, my men a few feet away in the lockup, when two MPs brought in a soldier, or rather half-carried him in, an MP on each arm. The man had dark hair and olive skin. Hispanic or Filipino, I guessed. His hair was full of dust and his fatigue pants torn. The MPs sat him down on a bench.

"Are you going to be quiet now?" one of the MPs said to him.

The soldier's face, I now noticed, was wet with tears, sweat, and mucus. He had a bloody nose.

Suddenly, he got up from the bench, turned around, and began beating his hands on the plywood wall behind him, yelling in a high-pitched voice, "Sons of bitches, you fuckin' sonsabitches!"

One of the MPs grabbed his arms and turned him around. The other slapped him across the face. Then, as if remembering that an officer was watching, that MP turned to me and said, "He pulled a .45 on us on Highway One, sir. We don't like to be too rough on these guys, they got it so bad in the field. But you can only take so much of their crap."

The prisoner started screaming in Spanish. The MP raised a hand, and the prisoner dropped his head and started muttering. I heard individual English words—"fuckin' die, fuckin' kill . . ."

The desk sergeant got my men out of the cell finally. Higgins came out wearing a big grin, as if he were very pleased with himself. I told him to wipe that grin off his face. When we got outside, the soldier was yelling again, and Higgins started laughing about this latest caper of his, thinking of course that I was just playing the game back inside the jailhouse. "Shut up," I said. He sulked for several days afterward.

About a month before, a hootch at Lieutenant Johnson's radio research detachment had been hit by a mortar round. One soldier had been badly wounded. Colonel Riddle had gone to survey the damage. I was called in to Chu Lai to see him and receive some new orders or, as he would have it, old ones. He said that Lieutenant Johnson's man wouldn't have been hurt at all, hardly, if the hootch had been properly sandbagged, and he'd been telling Lieutenant Johnson for months to get his hootches sandbagged. Didn't everyone damn well remember his orders about that?

I studied his face as he spoke. I suppose I might have tried to imagine his life and how he'd arrived at his present state, but to do that would have been to imagine myself like him, and perhaps that seemed all too easy to do. So I simply said, "Yes, sir," and, back at my detachment, started filling new sandbags, shoveling for an hour or more each day, bare-backed in the sun, streaming sweat. One or another of the men, usually Schulzie, came out and helped me sometimes. I said once or twice to them that they ought to be filling sandbags, too, but I didn't feel like giving them orders to do it. I imagined, briefly, that they'd see me working and be inspired by my example. Actually, I liked the mindless, heavy work, shoveling bags full, then tying them up, alone in the sun, outside the lounge, hearing beer cans hiss open. It made the days go by.

When Spikes finally returned, weeks later than he was supposed to, he told me, face alight, that he'd met a clerk in Okinawa who had managed to lose his orders temporarily, extending his leave. I smiled. "Number one, Stoney." But actually I felt hurt that he hadn't wanted to come back right away and help me.

The men had complained about the way I'd been treating Rose. He'd been chattering away in operations with a rifle in his hands, banging the butt down on the floor to emphasize a point. The rifle went off, and the bullet missed me by only a few inches. I didn't say anything. I just walked away. I'd mostly spoken sarcastically to him since then. Actually, the same men who complained about the way I treated Rose were downright cruel to him. This wasn't strange, of course. Criminals tend to feel indignant when cops break the law. A lieutenant was supposed to be fair to everyone.

But I resented their hypocrisy. My men had a habit of going off to the ville in the afternoon and coming back half an hour or an hour late when Rose was the commo op on duty. Rose said to me one night, "It ain't fair, Lieutenant."

When the overdue commo op returned, in the dusk, I went out and met him by the truck.

"You're late for duty. You made Rose work an hour extra."

The offending commo op had been the one who first heated up my shaving water. "Hey, no biggie, Lieutenant," he said.

I felt my upper lip curl. "If you do it again, I'm going to give you an Article Fifteen," I said.

That night in the lounge Spikes addressed me as "sir." I got him aside and asked him what was wrong.

"An Article Fifteen? That's pretty hard."

"I was pissed," I said.

He looked away. "Well, I didn't like it."

A couple of weeks later, the company commander insisted that Spikes return to Chu Lai and that I receive a new buck sergeant. Neither Spikes nor I objected. We shook hands. He said, "See ya around, Tracy." Just as well, I thought. Except for Schulzie, he was the only one by then who still called me by my first name.

SHORT

———||———

THE NEW COLONEL INVITED ME FOR DINNER at the field grade officers' mess. I told a few stories of the old days here in LZ Bayonet. I told the colonel that he'd had a predecessor who sometimes made me feel like the messengers in Shakespeare's **Antony and Cleopatra** whom the queen would punish for bringing her bad news. He laughed. Not caring if you make a good impression often helps you make one. All through the meal the provost marshal kept trying to question me about the metal roof that had gone missing from my detachment when we'd torn down the surplus hootch.

"I fail to see, Lieutenant, how someone could take an entire roof off one of your buildings and you not notice it."

"I know it, sir. I've been wondering the same thing."

I had a clear memory of Pancho and the other men from Baldy stripping off the metal. Even in his absence, Pancho remained a presence. And then, late in April, I got a call from Chu Lai. Pancho was due to return from his second R & R and would have only a week or so left in country when he got back. Evidently, he wanted to spend that time at my detachment. Did I have a problem with that?

"No, I guess not," I said.

THE COMPANY'S FIRST SERGEANT HAD FINISHED his tour some time ago. A new "top" had arrived, and the word on him had traveled fast from the enlisted men in Chu Lai to mine. They said this new first sergeant, Sergeant Harb, measured the men's mustaches and sideburns with a ruler to make sure they weren't longer than regulation size. They also said he'd lengthened the workday of the men back at the company headquarters, mainly by making them paint the company's hootches when they got off duty. I'd also heard about a commotion back at the company, something about a booby trap being found in the new first sergeant's hootch, and maybe some people thought Pancho was involved somehow. But I rejected all rumors out of hand now, and I went to Chu Lai as little as possible, so I didn't hear the whole story.

The new first sergeant came to visit us on a hot afternoon at the end of April; he was a skinny, leathery-looking man with a southern accent. He told me he was going to "he'p me out." He was going to help me decide which of our hootches we should paint first. I wondered to myself if this had something to do with Major Great. Word must have spread. **They** thought they could do as they pleased with me now. And they probably could have, except that by this time I'd have been the one who did most of the painting.

I was standing there in the sun, sweat was rolling into my eyes, and the first sergeant was smiling and I was smiling back at him, trying to think of a way to outmaneuver him, but wasn't coming up with anything. And then, glancing over the first sergeant's shoulder, I saw a deuce and a half stirring up dust out on the base camp street. The truck pulled in, and a red mailbag came out of the back, followed by a short, trim, black-haired figure in gold-framed sunglasses. The first sergeant was still talking away at me. I went on smiling at him, while from the corner of my eye, I watched Pancho saunter over toward us.

"Hey, Lieutenant!" He punched my arm. "I just got back from Taipei." He was grinning. "Man, it feels shitty bein' back in the ass-licking lifer Army, doesn't it, sir?" He laughed, and then, brushing his hair off his forehead, he made a quarter turn and said, "First Sergeant Harb! I didn't see ya! How you doin', First Sergeant?"

Harb glowered. "Fine till you got here," he muttered.

Clearly, there was something between them, some history I hadn't witnessed. Standing there on that baked and dusty yellow ground, I thought my hands might be shaking if I took them out of my pockets, because I felt so nervously excited and helpless to prevent whatever was about to happen. And in my mind I made one of those vows: I'm going to remember this.

The first sergeant was glaring at Pancho. Pancho was grinning at him. "Hey, First Sergeant! You're short!" Pancho cried. "I'm short, too! Maybe we'll go back on the same plane together!" Pancho laughed his hearty-sounding laugh, his round chest bouncing.

He went right on: "Yeah, I'm gettin' out of this flatdick Army, going to Fort Home. Maybe I'll come and see ya when I get out." Pancho lifted a hand. Did the first sergeant flinch? With the hand, Pancho again brushed his sleek, black hair, much longer than it should have been, off his forehead. "You live on . . ." Pancho rattled off the first sergeant's home address. He'd probably gotten it from a clerk-typist friend. "Yeah, maybe I will. Maybe I'll come and see you after I get out, First Sergeant. Got any kids?"

The scene, as I preserved it, dissolved soon afterward. Pancho sauntered away, calling in an alarmingly loud and cheerful voice to the other men that he was **back,** but not for long because he was **short,** so short he was afraid that when he got out of bed in the morning someone would step on him. And meanwhile, the first sergeant was saying something to me about having to get on down the road to headquarters, and he'd get back to me about painting the hootches.

Briefing the new brigade commander, I felt as if I were sleepwalking, it was all so familiar. Every morning I'd hear Pancho sounding off inside the EM hootch. "Short! I'm so short my feet don't touch the floor when I get out of my rack!" Doubly short, doubly enviable, because his DEROS was the same as his ETS, his estimated date of separation from the Army. He'd cry out, "ET-fucking-S-ing!" I had noticed in the mirror that my hairline had receded, and the boils on my shoulders would not go away. I'd visited the brigade dispensary, and a pleasant young doctor there had told me that the best thing to do for the boils was to DEROS. As for my slightly receding hairline, there was nothing at all to be done. "But it **is** a sign of virility," he'd added. "If that's any consolation." I'd made the mistake of telling Pancho my worries about my hair. Every time I ran into him around the detachment now, he'd say, "Short, Lieutenant. Hey, how's your hair?" Then he'd laugh and saunter off, saying, "Shaky." I was asleep in my hootch when he left for Fort Home.

I went on a second R & R, alone this time, and to Sydney, Australia. Round-eyed girls didn't meet me at the plane. I tried to pick one up who was tending bar. I even took my glasses off to talk to her. She agreed to meet me later that night on a street corner. I stood there for an hour, then wandered into another bar, where I got conned in a shell game, an actual shell game—but I complained to the manager and got my money back. I spent most of the rest of that R & R in my hotel room.

On the flight back to Vietnam, I sat beside an infantry lieutenant from the brigade. When I mentioned Colonel Mahoney, he told me that some grunts used to take shots at the colonel's chopper. The man was a lunatic, he said. The colonel would actually drop notes from his helicopter to squads and platoons down on the ground. He'd do this instead of simply giving them orders over the radio.

I said I thought I might know the reason for

that, but I didn't try to explain. Mostly I listened, raptly, to the lieutenant's stories, of the many deprivations of grunts, of the suicidal missions his commanders tried to assign his platoon, of his efforts to keep his men safe. I might have doubted some of this, except that several of his men were riding in the back of the plane, and when we got off they eyed me suspiciously and crowded around him, each one, I recall, giving him a manly punch on the arm, as if each felt it was necessary to touch him.

When I came back to my detachment, I had only three weeks left. One of the men, a commo op, had only three days. After dark, I wandered into the operations hootch and found him furiously typing out a message to company headquarters. I looked over his shoulder. THIS UNIT IS UNDER ATTACK. THIS UNIT IS UNDER ATTACK. The usual instruments were playing in the night, insects and big and little guns, but all the shells were outgoing.

"**Don't** send that message."

Another story often told, probably in all wars, was the one about the soldier who died with only a day or two left in country. I understood the commo op's fearfulness. He probably was afraid not of getting injured or killed—after all, he was even younger than I—but of what that would mean: that he wouldn't get to go home.

I tried to remember the last time I'd feared for my physical safety. Maybe over six months before, on the night when some sappers got into the base camp. But they'd gone after the brigade staff and had managed only to blow a few harmless holes, one in the floor of the field grade officers' mess hall, one in the floor of the field grade officers' hootch, and one in the eardrum of the S-3, who took his wound philosophically. (He said of the sappers, "I'd give them an A for planning and an F for execution," and he smiled, a wad of cotton sticking out of one ear.) I realized I'd never been in real danger, and I had a feeling that I was going to regret it.

In early June a letter arrived addressed to "Lt. Col. John Tracy Kidder." It began without a salutation:

Short! Well Lt. how does it feel? Good I bet. Well Lt.

Sorry I have taken so long too write but I hate it, too write. Well I sorry I didn't wake you up when I left but you had such a long time too go and you were losing your hair I just didn't have the heart too wake you since I knew you needed your rest. Well How is everyone, Tex, Melvin and Schulzie and the new 05G (sucker).

Well I have heard in the paper that things go bad over there, I hope it's not true, but It's not my bag anymore.

Well I just hope all of you guys are fine and well. Well here's my address in case you need something. . . .

I'm staying home untill July then I go too D.C. too work for the CIA.

Well Bye for now don't forget write back and let me know how all is

Your friend
El Pancho

excuse the writing because this is the second letter I've written in a long time the other was to Harris

The tall, young lieutenant who arrived to take over my detachment carried a photo of the Porsche he had bought before leaving home, and he said friends wondered which he'd miss more, his young wife or his car. I tried to give him a good start, for a few days. But he had ideas of his own, and one day he told me politely that he understood how I felt about tearing down part of the operations hootch, but he was going to do it anyway. I shrugged and walked away. Fucking asshole, I thought. Coming in here, into **my** detachment, saying he's going to do things his way.

Screw him. The next morning he said he'd like to brief the colonel alone. Lying on my cot late in the morning for the first time in almost a year, I cheered up a little. Schulzie got me aside in the lounge later on and said, "This new guy lieutenant acts like a puke." I forget what the issue was—filling sandbags or painting hootches or getting haircuts.

I made a face for Schulzie's benefit. Then I shrugged. "Short," I said.

Schulzie got up early the morning I left for good. We shook hands. We exchanged home addresses. He said he'd look me up once he got out of the service and had dealt with his Army recruiter.

I still had a few days left in Chu Lai, and on one of them I, along with some other lieutenants, was to receive my Bronze Star. I thought a good monograph might be written about the debasement of medals during the Vietnam War. In ASA anyway, virtually every officer got one, just for showing up. In my mind, I was already halfway home, and I was preparing my new self. I told my company commander that during the ceremony I was going to wear a set of love beads I'd purchased.

"Please don't," he said.

I wasn't going to admit it to him, but he'd been good to me. I didn't wear the beads. The company, all the EM, had to stand in formation while the medals were pinned on. I accepted mine. I thought to myself, What a disgrace, making all these EM stand out in the sun.

And I grew a mustache. It was risky, I thought, as I trimmed it. Really risky. I had to go through Nha Trang on my way out of country. Colonel Riddle wouldn't like the mustache. Neither would Major Great. But they were both away when I passed through. I stayed with the other officers at the villa, built, I imagined, by the French. On the rooftop patio, over cocktails, the executive officer said, "Officers in the five-oh-nine Radio Research Group don't wear mustaches, Lieutenant Kidder."

I'd met this officer once before. He'd visited my detachment, but he'd said when he arrived, "I'm not interested in inspecting the men's quarters."

"Yes, sir," I said to him now. "But Army regulations permit mustaches."

He looked at me, and he smiled. Then he shook his head.

My last night there I shared a room with a soft-spoken lieutenant, another southerner. He told me he envied me the year I'd had. He'd been stuck here in Nha Trang the whole time. Early on, Colonel Riddle had called him "boy," and he'd lodged a formal complaint. Since then he'd been obliged to spend every evening running the movie projector for the colonel. "Nasty movies. I mean nasty," he said. "But I won't let him get to me," he drawled, and he smiled. I liked him as much as anyone I'd ever met in the Army, but I have misplaced his name, of course.

And then days of travel began again—airplanes with slings for seats and no windows, wooden benches in the back of a big truck and a view of tin-roofed shacks on the outskirts of Saigon, and strange bunks and olive-drab blankets at the transit camp where they fitted you with a khaki uniform and where, on the last day, I realized I lacked a garrison cap. I couldn't find one and had a dream on the perimeter of sleep that for the lack of a hat I wouldn't be allowed to go home. There was a bus in the dark before dawn, which I could have sworn was motoring through villages in France, and finally there was the Freedom Bird. A great cheer went up in the cabin when the wheels left the ground, and soon afterward there was another cheer, not quite as loud, and I wondered, groggily, what that second cheer was for, until I looked out the window and saw the coast of Vietnam passing below us. I turned to the soldier in the seat beside me. He seemed to be asleep. His eyes were closed. He was smiling.

A VISITOR

—‖—

ASOLDIER RETURNS FROM VIETNAM AND AT the airport runs into a bunch of antiwar demonstrators, who welcome him home by spitting on him. This became one of the most common stories from the war. I don't believe it actually happened very often—if it had, there would have been an alarming increase in mayhem at civilian airports. I think the tale acquired wide currency because it neatly expressed the feelings shared by a part of a generation of American boys.

For the minority who had seen combat, the myth surely expressed a figurative truth. Among them were the soldiers who came back permanently wounded and ended up in the wards of VA hospitals, some of which were rat-infested. There were the African American veterans I interviewed in Birmingham who had been promised vocational training in the Army and wound up in combat in Vietnam and now couldn't find jobs (one of whom said of his homecoming: "People didn't treat you no different. It was like, 'Hey, I ain't seen you in a **long** time. Where you been? You been in jail?"). And there were the former grunts who slipped back as quietly as they could into houses on suburban streets, carrying secrets that only their girlfriends and wives would discover, when they found the carving knife under the bed in the morning. But for the majority of the three million Americans who went to Vietnam, the REMFs, I think the myth spoke mainly about disappointed expectations.

I took a cab with a couple of majors from Travis Air Force Base to San Francisco Airport. On the way we passed the campus of Berkeley, long a principal site of antiwar fervor. "I went there," said one of the majors, gazing out the cab window. "It was a good place back then." Despising all majors now that I was heading home, I thought to myself that if **he** felt that way, Berkeley must have greatly improved.

Maybe if we'd stopped and walked around that

campus in our uniforms, we'd have found someone to spit on us. I wonder if I would have preferred that to the scene at the airport. Men and
women in suits, families on vacations. I kept
expecting that someone would accost me. I'd
heard the stories. In fact, no one seemed to notice
me. I wasn't offended, exactly. The camera had
started running again. Soldier returns home in
anonymity. He's been away a long time. He has
changed. At the same time, I didn't want anyone,
anyone at all, to see me in uniform. I felt
ashamed, of the uniform itself, of almost everything I could remember doing in it, and of everything people would think I had done in it but, sad
to say, I hadn't done. Meanwhile, I was happy. I
was going home. And I was still a little worried
that I hadn't been able to find a garrison cap.
Could an MP on patrol in the airport arrest me for
being slightly out of uniform?

SAM WAS WAITING FOR ME AT MY PARENTS' HOUSE.
We drank champagne and didn't talk about the
war. I went to Cambridge and stayed with David
Riggs. He told me, "You know, before you went to
Vietnam, I found a letter you wrote to your
brother. You must have dropped it in the hall outside my door." He smiled. He said he had
destroyed it after reading it. "I was afraid an

undergraduate would find it and have a nervous breakdown."

I called Mr. Fitzgerald from a pay phone. He invited me to lunch at his house the next afternoon. Of course, I didn't tell him this, but I wanted something from him, mainly hope for the novel I was going to write. He had prepared sandwiches. I'm not sure he made them himself, but I like to think that he did, and that he was responsible for cutting the crusts off the bread. It seemed a sweet gesture, a way of making me feel I was important to him. It also made him seem old, older than I'd remembered him.

Men landed on the moon for the first time during my thirty-day, post-Vietnam leave. I was riding in the car of a young woman whose surname I don't remember—if I did, I would write her a letter of apology—and we were driving toward Cape Cod, when the news came over the radio. "Bastards!" I yelled. "Why don't they leave the fucking moon alone!"

She said, "I think it's great. What's the matter with you?"

After leave I went to Fort Holabird, a post in Baltimore devoted to Army Intelligence, to serve the last months of my two-year enlistment. I was assigned to an African American colonel who needed someone to write up a short biographical essay about Nathan Hale, an early

American spy, supposedly the country's first intelligence officer. The colonel said he realized I'd been in Vietnam and didn't have much time left until my ETS. He was very kind. He told me I didn't have to come to the post, just write up a story about Hale that he could use for some upcoming ceremony. I lived in a houseboat with several intelligence officers I'd known at Infantry School at Fort Benning. But I got lonely there. So I put on my uniform and went to the post, and a colonel I'd never laid eyes on before stopped me on a path and made me stand at attention while he examined me. He ordered me to get a haircut. I went to the barbershop right away. And the next day I had to go to the post in uniform to get my pay, and the same colonel stopped me again.

"I thought I told you to get a haircut, Lieutenant."

"I did, sir."

"No, you didn't."

"Yes, sir, I did."

"I don't believe you."

I held my tongue while he examined my belt buckle. "This brass is turning green. Look at your shoes. What the hell do you think you're doing, Lieutenant?"

"I ETS in a month, sir," I said. The minute I said it I knew I'd made a bad mistake. How idiotic, to tell this powerful lifer I was about to leave the Army.

"You're not going to ETS or any other damn thing if you don't shape up, Lieutenant."

Fear, real fear, shot through me. I wanted to bite my fingernails. I think that, for the first time in my life, I had homicidal thoughts. The odd thing was I didn't feel angry. I felt that if this person stood in my way, I'd have to get him out of my way. Even odder, I thought that I had shined my brass. I thought I'd shined my shoes. Yet, looking down at my uniform later, I didn't see how I could have. I knew I'd gotten a haircut. This choleric colonel must know something about me, I thought. Maybe he knew something about me that I didn't know.

I didn't go back to the base again, not until my last day in the Army, when I had to visit its various offices for out-processing. At headquarters a clerk handed me a "Command Information Fact Sheet." I glanced through it, and, coming to the end, I read: "For some, the return to civilian life may make the Army seem remote; but some things from your service will be with you for-ever—not unpleasant things which the mind tends to reject—but good, worthwhile memories. If you were in Vietnam, such memories may include a village scene, a child, a girl, a buddy. . . ."

I tucked the pamphlet in among all the other

papers I'd collected. My last acts in the Army were administrative. Now I was done with them, released, finished with wearing a green suit. All that remained was a walk to the parking lot and the used sports car I'd bought with the pay I'd saved in Vietnam. The post was a warren of old brick buildings that reminded me of American high schools of a previous era. I was walking along an asphalt path, looking down at my shoes and watching shinier ones go by, when someone spoke to me.

"Lieutenant Kidder?"

I looked up, right into a face I knew I recognized, that ever so ordinary face, gold oak leaves on the collar of his greens. "Major Great."

He was staring at the left side of my chest, the place where soldiers wear those little ribbons that represent medals. I was wearing mine. He shook his head and made a short laugh, half a snort, half a cluck. "You've got your Bronze Star on upside down," he said. "Here, let me fix it."

"No, that's all right, sir. I'll do it myself."

"All right, Lieutenant."

I saluted him, he saluted back, and we went our separate ways.

I thought that I was done with him then and with all he represented for me. As I walked away, out of the Army, I thought of him walking the other way, pursuing his undistinguished career inside that vast, malfunctioning clockwork. I tried to imagine the life in front of him. Paperwork and acronyms and young men who wouldn't get dressed right. Too bad he wasn't a more prepossessing villain. But what a horrible life. Incomprehensible, really. And, of course, he probably walked off still shaking his head, thinking much the same thing about me.

I had planned to throw my hat in the air when I drove out of the gate of Fort Holabird, but I didn't feel like doing that when the time came. There wasn't much of an audience, only an MP, a private, in the guardhouse.

I took off my uniform when I got back to the houseboat. I was alone. I lit a fire in the Franklin stove and stuffed in my pants and shirt. They wouldn't burn. Finally I gave up and dropped them in the trash.

MARY ANNE CAME TO SEE ME AT MY PARENTS' house in Oyster Bay. I'd carried a photograph of her in my wallet to and from Vietnam. A picture taken on my father's catboat, when she was about sixteen. She didn't look much different now. Once again, she had the freckles near her nose that always appeared in summer. But the expression on her face wasn't mischievous. It was sad. We sat outside, the hem of her skirt spread on domesticated grass, beneath an immature dogwood tree. I knew she'd come to let me know that I wouldn't see her again. I felt a keening trying to escape from my throat, knowing that I would always miss her, the first girl I'd loved. A familiar doubleness came over me, as if inward tears split my vision so that in one half I was seeing myself suffering and enjoying the spectacle.

I knew she wanted to make a clean end. I might have made it easy for her if I had let myself remember all her gifts to me—not just the good times without number or her many kindnesses, but what she had awakened in me. She had enlarged my sense of life, both its sorrows and its joys. But I wanted this to cost her. I was going to tell her some of the contents of the unmailed letter I'd written before R & R. I'd say that when her letters stopped, I got so angry and cared so little about anything that I volunteered for dangerous missions, just so I could kill people. "I killed people because of you," I planned to say. I wasn't sure why, any more than I was sure why I'd saved that unmailed letter, or why it seemed romantic to be someone who had killed people. I picked at the grass and said that, after her letters dwindled, I did some terrible things, and then I stopped, ashamed.

She said, "I ruined everything, didn't I."

And then I realized that, for effect, the hint of a terrible war story was the best war story of all.

I FINISHED **IVORY FIELDS** ABOUT A YEAR LATER, IN Boston's South End, on the top floor of a building under renovation, where I got free room in return for unskilled labor.

I began the last chapter with a portrait based on Harris, a character I called Casey, a member of the now-deceased Lieutenant Dempsey's platoon. He's been wounded ("at that little fight we had down near Quang Ngai City"). An Army psychiatrist has decided Casey is no longer fit for combat duty. That particular psychiatrist always makes this diagnosis: "He thought that all combat soldiers belonged in nuthouses." Casey now works at the Chu Lai dump, known to soldiers as the "black plague." I'd seen the actual place, and the Vietnamese picking through the garbage. Casey has an epiphany there. He gives a kid his boots, then spends all his pay at the PX to buy more stuff to give away at the dump. He tells his nasty boss, a spec. 5 named McGuire, "Man, watch out. One of these days you come back and this truck's gonna be gone. It's going to be **gone**. I might have to give it away." I wrote: "Casey's old white eyes watched McGuire turn away. He smiled secretly. And that is not all."

Seated at a makeshift desk in my temporary garret lodgings, I wrote: "Although that is not all and many fates still hung in the balance, including that of Ivory Fields, it must do for now. Larry Dempsey's body is home and underground. There is an end. May his soul rest in peace."

At the bottom of the page I wrote, "1970." Finishing, I recall, seemed like a good way to begin a new decade.

THE WORKING CLASS OF AMERICA HAD LONG been among the war's staunchest supporters, at least in part for a tragic reason: It was their sons, mainly, who were obliged to go to Vietnam and who did most of the fighting and dying there, and one could not expect them easily to disown the cause to which they'd sacrificed so much. But over the years, memories altered, softened, faded. For many, even some of those directly responsible for it, the whole enterprise came to be viewed as misbegotten at best. Others held fast to the notion that if only it weren't for "politics," the war could have been won. But no one blamed the veterans anymore.

Almost all the movies about Vietnam, the ones I saw anyway, treated American soldiers sympathetically—and all but a few made war seem attractive, even the movies that didn't mean to,

maybe those especially. By the early 1980s, I
noticed that mentioning my service in Vietnam
often produced long faces and murmurs of sympathy. It still does on occasion, from people of
various ages. Sometimes I'm happier if I don't
answer and remain in the warmth of the miscon-
ception. Usually I say that I didn't have a bad
time, that I and most of the soldiers who went
there weren't in anything like combat. And sometimes I feel transported into memories of the kind
of soldier I was, and this in turn is apt to lead me
into silent colloquy with literary critics. Now and
then, over the years in which I've written and pub-
lished nonfiction books, I've been accused of
being too soft on the people I've tried to depict. I
want to say to my critics that if the flaws in those
people were obvious to them, they were also obvious to me. But, I want to add, I'd like to avoid
being judgmental, and I have reason to try.

I'm a decade more than twice as old as the lieutenant who commanded the Radio Research
detachment with the 198th Light Infantry
Brigade of the disgraced and long disbanded
Americal Division. For me, almost all that
remains of the colonels and majors and captains I
met, and of the enlisted men I lived with, are
memories. I lost touch with all of them—or
nearly all.

Over the years, from time to time, I heard from

Pancho. In 1970, after I'd moved to Boston, he called my parents' house. My mother described him as "a strange young man, but very polite." Twice over the next decade he called my home in western Massachusetts, but I was away on each occasion. Near the end of 1985, I found an envelope in my mailbox addressed to "Shakey Kidder," with a return address in Saudi Arabia. He had written inside, "Shakey & Family Merry Christmas!" Then, one morning in 1986, he came to visit me. Unexpectedly, which I suppose was to be expected. The phone rang, and a familiar voice said, "Hey, Lieutenant Colonel Kidder."

"Pancho!" I said.

I heard that low, sneaky laugh. "Heh heh. You remember my name." Actually, he said, someone had given him the nickname when he got to Vietnam. No one had ever called him Pancho before or since, but he didn't mind if I did.

A few minutes later he arrived in a rental car. He'd put on a lot of weight, but I think I would have recognized him on a street. We sat around my house for a while, comparing memories. I asked him, for instance, if he remembered the guy who refused to believe he couldn't travel at the speed of light and how dour he'd become in his last weeks at the detachment.

"Yeah, something happened towards the end," Pancho said. "He was leaving, I don't know. Maybe he was getting sad. That happened to a lot of people. When I left, I almost re-upped."

"You **did?**"

He was in an out-processing center in Oakland, and a bunch of officers and sergeants were trying to get ETS-ing soldiers to reenlist. "Here I am, a young kid, no real education, and all I know is the Army. But then, it was funny, this lieutenant, he said to me, 'Tie your tie. Your tie ain't right, trooper.' I'm getting out in one minute and they're makin' me tie my tie again, and I'm saying to myself, 'Get out, dummy, don't stay around.' "

He'd gone back to St. Louis, his hometown, he said. He worked there for a month in a grease factory. "Pushin' fifty-five-gallon drums of oil around. I'm serious. This is hard labor, slave labor." Through a series of coincidences, he got a job working for the CIA. "So I'm being briefed and the guy's going through all the old code words and I noticed one old one, the same on the message we lost. SUNDAE I think was the word. I said, 'Hey this doesn't exist anymore.' He said, 'That's right, some fool lost a message or something.' I said, 'You're looking at him.' "

I let the story go. "You know, Pancho," I said, "they could have busted you for losing that message."

"They couldn't have busted **you**," he said. "You were a second lieutenant. You couldn't go any lower, could you? They could have promoted you, and then busted you."

We laughed.

He said he'd quit the CIA when he found himself deskbound. Soon afterward he'd gone back to Vietnam as a civilian, and worked there for four years as an electronics technician for military subcontractors.

I said it must have been frightening near the end of the war.

"Yeah, okay," he said. "Places got blown up, people tried to rob you now and then. But I guess I'm a lucky guy. Most people didn't bother me because I'd just look at them and I guess they figured this guy might just do something. And I always carried my weapon where I could get at it and I carried two grenades just in case, 'cause you don't know. I'm not that brave of a man. I was pretty lucky. I was up with Air America, just the pilot and me flying to places where nobody else was at, and it was a little scary sometimes, but then you're young, you say to yourself, Ah, don't worry about it, just keep movin', just keep goin' forward."

Subsequent jobs had taken him to Morocco and Egypt and Saudi Arabia. He was in Iran, he said, when the Shah fell. "I stayed there for the revolution. In fact, I kind of helped them a little bit. But that's another story."

We went out to lunch, in the college town of Northampton, at a rather fancy restaurant now vanished, called Beardsley's. We sat in a booth— the benches in the booths, it's important to say, had cushions on them. He clarified some memories.

"Okay, what happened was, we got together, all of us. I was the ringleader." He paused. "Lunch is on me for this, by the way." He laughed. "I planned this down to—I even emptied out your fire extinguisher. Then I opened up the back of your latrine and poured the kerosene and continued to pour it on, and then I waited until the whole latrine was burning. So then I went ahead and I came into your hootch and you were kind of half asleep, and you came running out and you grabbed the fire extinguisher and you went out there. **Shhh.** It didn't work." He laughed and laughed. Then he said, "It was not meant to be mean to you. The problem was we didn't have the manpower to run two latrines."

He talked about his past, and I realized with surprise how little I'd known of the basic facts of Pancho. He'd grown up in a proper Chicano family, where instant obedience to one's father was law. One day when he was eighteen, his father told him to cut the grass. The right thing to say would have been "**Como me mandas**"—in effect, "Yes, sir." But Pancho said, "In a minute," and his father slapped him. "I walked back in the house, took a duffel bag and the five dollars I had, and I didn't say a word to my parents, and I walked down to the office of the Army recruiter."

He told me: "I was just a rebellious person, and I refused to bend into certain things. In the Army, I knew if I didn't cross the line, they couldn't do anything to me anyway. Send me to Vietnam, right?"

Had there been something between him and that second first sergeant? I asked.

"Yeah, he wanted my AK-47."

"I didn't know you had an AK-47. I thought you just had that Swedish K."

"Oh, you remember that? No, I had an AK-47, too. The first sergeant wanted it, and I wouldn't give it to him. He went out to get the MPs. The other problem was, the other guys, they were egging me on. Your honor, Pancho. They're all talking. So I left. I snuck around. The first sergeant had his own hootch there in Chu Lai. I said, I'm gonna fix this sonofabitch. I took a grenade. I always carried grenades, and one of them was a dummy, which I always carried, just in case I wanted to do something to somebody. So I went ahead and I wired up his door. The next day they had a full alert because they thought the VC had come in there. Remember that?"

"I remember something sort of like that."

"That was me." He laughed.

It was one of the laughs I remembered, from deep in the chest, a throbbing laugh. I had a question I wasn't sure I wanted answered. But the sound of that laugh was reassuring. "Do you remember when that major came? Major Great? There was this horrible inspection and I fell all apart?"

He laughed again, just as heartily.

"I'm curious as to how I appeared to you," I went on. "It won't hurt my feelings. Don't worry. It was a long time ago."

"You gotta remember something," he said. "I wouldn't have wrote you a letter saying Lieutenant Colonel Kidder for nothin'. I personally liked you, that was the main thing. If I like somebody, they're gonna know fast enough. We were young. I'd already been in the Army a lot longer than you. I was gettin' out, I knew they couldn't do anything to me as long as I didn't go over the edge. Sometimes I've actually thought about some of the things we did to you. For me, the most famous was burning your latrine. I put the snake over you. I used to sneak up on you."

He laughed, his shaky laugh this time—"heh heh"—and said, "I had a lot of freedom, simply because I made it that way."

We went on talking, and at one point he said, "I never had any great plans to being anybody, but when I'm involved in something, I'm always scheming, because I don't like things to be the normal everyday drudgery."

As he continued, saying that he wanted to travel more, that it was in his blood, it occurred to me that he had just stated the essential difference between us, back when we'd been soldiers. He had wanted to have an interesting life. I had wanted to be interesting.

We lingered over coffee. Finally, it seemed as though there was nothing more to say. We got up to leave. Sliding out of the booth, I knocked the cushion off the bench. It fell beneath the table. I got down on one knee, stuck my hand under the table, and was groping for the cushion, when I heard Pancho say, musingly to himself, "Same old lieutenant."

ABOUT THE AUTHOR

TRACY KIDDER graduated from Harvard and studied at the University of Iowa. He has won the Pulitzer Prize, the National Book Award, the Robert F. Kennedy Award, and many other literary prizes. The author of **Mountains Beyond Mountains, Home Town, Old Friends, Among Schoolchildren, House,** and **The Soul of a New Machine,** Kidder lives in Massachusetts and Maine.